D0615934

Dog Tricks
Step by Step

Revised Edition

Dog Tricks
Step by Step

Revised Edition

Mary Ann Rombold Zeigenfuse
Illustrated by Jan Walker

HOWELL
BOOK
HOUSE

New York

Copyright © 1997, 2003 by Mary Ann Rombold Zeigenfuse and Jan Walker

Howell Book House

Published by Wiley Publishing, Inc., New York, NY

For general information on our other products and services or to obtain technical support please contact our Customer Care Department within the U.S. at 800-762-2974, outside the U.S. at 317-572-3993 or fax 317-572-4002.

Wiley also publishes its books in a variety of electronic formats. Some content that appears in print may not be available in electronic books.

ISBN: 0-7645-6428-5

Cataloging-in-Publication Data available from the Library of Congress.

Manufactured in the United States of America
10 9 8 7 6 5 4 3 2 1
Revised Edition

Cover design by Holly Wittenberg

Book production by Wiley Publishing, Inc. Composition Services

*In Memory of my Dad, William M. Rombold and
my dog, Bosé. Dad was the first trickster in my life.
Bosé was "the wind beneath my wings."*

Contents

Acknowledgments

There was a time when I thought I might have been adopted. Not that that would have been bad, but it seemed to me that I was the only one in my family who was infatuated with dogs. I had only one dream as a child and that was to own a dog. This dream was not shared by any other member of my family. I thought I was a misfit. This thought stayed with me until only recently. On a visit to my home town, I went to see my Uncle Fred and Aunt Ann. Uncle Fred was my father's older brother and one of my favorite people growing up. One of the reasons was that he always had a dog, so to visit Uncle Fred meant also to play with a dog. During the visit, Uncle Fred was catching me up on the family news; this information was presented with love and interest, but no pictures. Then he started to tell me about a dog who lived in the neighborhood where he and my aunt summered in Florida. He told me how he walked the dog every day and what a great friend this dog had become. You guessed it: This is when the pictures came out. He had pictures of the dog walking with him and of the dog alone. My heart just squeezed. It was like coming home. In my home I could show you snapshots of every dog I know, but don't ask to see pictures of my friends and relatives. Those would take a lot more time to put my hands on. So, Uncle Fred, thank you for letting me be part of your family.

The other important people in my life who have made me feel like family are Jack and Wendy Volhard. They understand dogs, people, and how to communicate with both. They are true teachers. They want to give everyone everything they know and have to offer. They have taught me so much and have taken me under their wing. At the same time, they have pushed me to be what I can and to do it on my own. Without them as my mentors, I wouldn't be writing to you, and I couldn't have been here. Thank you, Jack and Wendy, for "adopting" me.

Then there are the dogs. So many dogs have taught me so much, sometimes baffling me, sometimes humoring me, but always allowing me into their lives and their hearts. I meet many dogs every day, and each is so honest in approach and so willing to play along with whatever I dish out. I thank them all and look forward to meeting tomorrow's dogs.

Some of the dogs in my life are pictured in this book. They are:

- Nipper-T, a Yorkshire Terrier, owned by myself and my husband, Robert Zeigenfuse.

- Clay, a yellow Labrador, owned by Casey Eckert.

- Lil Bit, an Australian Shepherd, owned by Ann Keller.

- Sparky, an All-American, owned by Diane and Allen Haughey.

- Sadie, a chocolate Labrador, owned by Mary Margaret Sterling.

- Orco, a Border Collie, owned by Ann Keller.

- Zoo, an All-American, owned by Diane and Allen Haughey.

- Fresco, a black Labrador, owned by Barb Koetsier.

- Muppy, an All-American, owned by Pat Graham.

- Chica, owned by Monica Udvardy and Thomas Hakånsson.

- Shana, a Border Collie, owned by Sharon Shepard.

- Zack, a Viszla, owned by Lisa Hamblen.

I would also like to thank my sister, Tamara Yohannes, who allowed me to bounce everything off her for this book. This was a true gift to me, because as I said before, I am the only real dog person in my family. Thanks, Tamara.

Introduction

First and foremost, dogs are our companions. They bring us joy, and as any proud dog person can attest, showing off our dogs to the world is a whole lot of fun. We can show them off for their good looks, for their charm, and for their talents and skills.

This book will explain how to highlight your dog's natural talents, enhance her instinctive behaviors, and possibly even make your dog famous by performing new and attention-getting tricks. The fame may only reach as far as your living room, or it may take you all the way to Hollywood. Either way, it is sure to bring your dog deep into your heart.

Capitalize on your dog's talents.

Most dogs will be able to learn *all* of the tricks in this book. By using the Canine Personality Test that follows, you will see which tricks are best suited for *your* individual dog and which ones will be easiest for her to learn. This test is your very own recipe for built-in success.

Would you like your dog to Bob for Apples or Sneeze on command? What if your dog could Wake Up the Kids or go Trick or Treating with you? My personal favorite is a dog who can Find the Remote Control.

Whatever it is that you want your dog to learn, you can teach her. With help from this book, you will learn the important steps to teach your dog just about anything. This book is all about having fun while you and your dog practice tricks. The only limitation is your imagination.

Make your dog a star.

Chapter 1

Getting Started

You can start teaching your dog his very first trick right away. You will need a start to the trick—this is called the *command*—and you will need an end to the trick. This is called the *release*. You can praise throughout your dog's performance, so don't use praise words as your release. The release word should be something like "OK." This will signal to your dog that work is now finished, and he can have a reward. The reward can be anything your dog likes: petting, a treat, or play time with his favorite toy. Whatever reward you give your dog, he really needs to know that his work is finished when you say, "OK."

LET'S RECAP

Each trick has:

1 A **Command,** which tells your dog what to do.

2 **Praise** during your dog's performance.

3 A **Release Word** to end the trick.

4 A **Reward** or something else that your dog likes.

The release ends the trick.

WAG YOUR TAIL

An easy first trick that all dogs can learn—even those with just a stub of a tail—is to wag their tails on command. Your dog's tail probably already wags in response to pleasant words from you. You can take this natural expression of happiness and turn it into a trick that your dog can perform on command. By starting with this trick, you will also practice using a command word and a release word. Be sure to praise your dog while he works. You should capitalize on your relationship with your dog—you're a team now.

First decide on the *command* that you want to use. It can be something simple like: "Bingo, wag your tail," or a more philosophical question: "Bingo, are you a happy dog?" Once you make up your mind, stick to it for consistency's sake. You want your dog to learn your command. Say the command with a lot of enthusiasm in your voice, using a happy, almost squeaky tone. Your dog will get excited and respond to your attention with his tail wagging. *Praising your dog's performance will keep his tail wagging.* You can then release your dog by saying "OK" and giving him a treat or a petting session. Then try it again.

Praising your dog's performance will keep his tail wagging.

1 **Command** in a high and happy voice: "Are you a happy dog?"

2 **Praise** to get the tail really moving.

3 **Release** by saying, "OK."

4 **Reward** your dog with a cookie or petting session.

Most likely your dog will get excited and want to do this trick over and over again. Remember that you are trying to label your dog's chosen behavior, so be sure your command sounds clear and different from other things that you say.

This is a **Prey Drive** trick because of the motivational, high-pitched tone of voice. Prey Drive behaviors are based on the instinct to hunt, kill, and feed. **Pack Drive** is also necessary for this trick because it expresses the bond between you and your dog. Pack Drive is based on social interaction with both humans and other animals.

YOUR DOG'S PERSONALITY

If you have more than one dog—or have known more than one dog—you already appreciate that each dog has a very different personality. One dog may like to cuddle more than the other. One may like to play ball while the other doesn't. And one may guard the house while the other runs in the opposite direction when he is approached by a stranger. What makes individual dogs so different?

Every dog, including yours, was born with a partially predetermined personality. But your dog's experiences since birth have helped to mold that personality. Such experiences include how his mother raised him and his littermates and at what age each dog left the litter. Your dog's experiences influence the way that he looks at the world and how he reacts to it. It's incredible, but you can actually take a test and figure out how your dog will react to his environment. This test will quickly determine what your dog's Drives are—and will give you insight into the personality characteristics you are most likely to see in your dog.

Remember—the way your dog reacts to the world is instinctive. Instinctive behaviors can be broken into three categories or Drives:

- Prey Drive

- Pack Drive

- Defense Drive

These Drives are thought to be natural talents because dogs come preprogrammed with them. But it's the concentration of each Drive that makes up a dog's individual personality.

By testing your dog, you can see how high the Drives are in each category. You can then determine how your dog might look at the world. This will help you understand how your dog learns so that you can have an idea of the tricks and exercises that will be easier—or harder—for him to know and accomplish.

You can determine how your dog views the world.

THE PERSONALITY TEST

Let's see how your dog's personality is arranged. Each category in this test has a set of questions. Answer *honestly* what you think your dog would do if he found himself in any of the following situations. If your dog would *almost always* react a certain way, give yourself 10 points; for *sometimes*, give yourself 5 points, and if you believe that your dog would hardly ever do what the question asks, score 0 points. *Points are neither bad nor good.* The total score simply gives you the proportions of the three Drives that your dog possesses. Note that Defense Drive is split into two categories—each category gets a separate set of questions.

Canine Personality Test

Always: 10   Sometimes: 5   Hardly Ever: 0

Personality/Behavior Questions

Prey Drive

Does your dog:

1   Sniff the ground or the air a lot?   _____

2   Get excited by moving objects, such as bikes or squirrels?   _____

3	Stalk cats, other dogs, or things in the grass?	_____
4	Bark in a high-pitched voice when he's excited?	_____
5	Pounce on toys?	_____
6	Shake and "kill" toys?	_____
7	Steal food or garbage?	_____
8	Like to carry things?	_____
9	Wolf down food?	_____
10	Enjoy digging and burying things?	_____

Total for Prey Drive Section: _____

Recognize your dog's capabilities, and answer
each question honestly.

Pack Drive

Does your dog:

1	Get along with other dogs?	_____
2	Get along with people?	_____
3	Bark when left alone?	_____
4	Solicit petting or snuggle with you?	_____
5	Like to be groomed?	_____
6	Seek eye contact with you?	_____

Jumping up to greet people
is part of Pack Drive.

7   Follow you around like a shadow?   _____

8   Play a lot with other dogs?   _____

9   Jump up to greet people?   _____

10 Show reproductive behaviors, such as courting
    or mounting other dogs?   _____

    Total of Pack Drive Answers: _____

Defense/Fight Drive

Does your dog:

1   Stand his ground or investigate strange objects and sounds? _____

2   Like to play tug of war games to win?   _____

3   Bark or growl in a deep tone?   _____

4   Guard his territory?   _____

5   Guard his food and toys?   _____

6   Dislike being petted?   _____

7   Guard his owner(s)?   _____

8   Dislike being groomed or bathed?   _____

9   Like to fight with other dogs?   _____

10 Get picked on by other dogs
    (either now or when he was young)?   _____

    Total of Defense/Fight Responses: _____

Guarding is part of Defense/Fight Drive.

Defense/Flight Drive

Does your dog:

1   Run away from new situations?   _____

2   Hide behind you when he's unable to cope?   _____

3   Act fearful in unfamiliar situations?   _____

4   Tremble or whine when he's unsure?   _____

5   Crawl or turn upside down when he's been reprimanded? _____

6   Reluctantly come close to you when called?   _____

7   Have difficulty standing still while being groomed?   _____

8   Cringe when someone strange bends over him?   _____

9   Urinate during greeting behavior?   _____

10 Tend to bite when he's cornered?   _____

Total of Defense/Flight Responses: _____

This dog exhibits Defense/Fight by confronting an intruder . . .

As you can tell from the questions themselves, each category says a little bit about your dog's psychological makeup. Pack Drive shows your dog's willingness to be part of a pack or a group that includes you. Prey Drive displays the instincts that helped dogs get food when they lived in the wild. Defense/Fight shows just that—behaviors associated with your dog's defending his territory or space. Defense/Flight shows a dog's concern for his well being—and that he would probably rather leave the scene during a stressful situation if he could, just as you might wish at times that the floor would open up and swallow you.

With few exceptions, dogs will have some of each Drive. Dogs need all the Drives to survive in Nature. And even though we now provide their food and shelter, dogs still need Prey Drive to play and retrieve. We secure our dogs' safety, but they continue to require Defense/Fight Drive so that they can cope with the pressures of hard work—like learning new tricks! And all dogs need Pack Drive so that they can live in harmony with us. The need for Defense/Flight is not really evident in domestic situations, but if dogs have a lot of Defense/Flight Drive, it is important to know it—the way we act towards a dog with a lot of Flight Drive will make or break him. A dog with high Flight Drive can be easily stressed and may experience constant turmoil if he isn't provided with a consistent and stable environment.

The level of each Drive is what determines your dog's personality. Any number above 50 is considered high. Obviously, the closer to 100, the higher the Drive. A dog can be high in all the Drives: Prey, Pack, and Defense (either Fight or Flight), or a dog can be high in only one or in none. A score below 30 is considered low in any Drive.

Being low in a Drive is not necessarily bad—and being high in a Drive is not necessarily good. The numbers simply teach you about your dog. True, some Drives are more desirable for certain tasks than others. High Fight Drive is needed for a task that requires a dog with a lot of confidence to work alone, for instance, a guard dog or a guide dog. High Pack Drive is desirable for a family pet or a therapy dog. And high Prey Drive is needed for a good herding dog.

... while this dog exhibits Defense/Flight Drive by hiding from an intruder.

As mentioned, a score over 50 is considered high, and too much of a good thing is not so desirable either. A high Prey Drive dog may not be able to concentrate if leaves in nearby trees are rustling. Learn your dog's Drives so that you can be prepared for any situation you put your dog into. If you know what to expect from your dog, you won't be surprised or disappointed by his actions. You will easily anticipate your dog's behavior once you know his Personality Profile.

Each trick in this book is marked as being easier for one Drive or the other. For easy success, start with a Drive that is marked as *your dog's highest.* Then, move on to the other Drives. Remember, *anything can be taught to any dog.* It is just a matter of understanding what Drive your dog is strongest in and what Drive you want your dog to be—and knowing how to get there. Making it fun for you and your dog is the key.

It is important to be aware of your body language when you deal with dogs. When you lean forward and over a dog, it places that dog into Defense Drive. Dogs high in Flight might run or flip over on their backs. If you lean backwards with your hands up, you may put a dog into Prey Drive. This

Guide dogs need a lot of confidence, which they get from Defense/Fight Drive.

is very stimulating and can be helpful when you're trying to get a dog to jump over something. A neutral posture with a smile on your face puts dogs into Pack Drive.

Body Language Signals You Need To Be Aware Of

A hug can elicit Pack Drive.

To put a dog into **PACK DRIVE:**

1   Use a **neutral posture**. Bend *neither* forward nor backwards.

2   Wear a **smile** on your face.

3   Use a **pleasant tone** of voice.

4   **Pet** or touch the dog warmly.

To put a dog into **PREY DRIVE:**

1   **Lean backwards,** away from your dog.

2   **Wave** or move your **arms.**

3   Use a **high pitch** tone of voice.

4   **Run with** your dog—or **throw something,** such as food, to your dog.

To put a dog into **DEFENSE DRIVE:**

1   Lean over or **towards** your dog.

2   Use a **deep**—not necessarily loud—tone of **voice.**

3   **Apply collar pressure** or use a leash with pressure.

Running with your dog can bring out his Prey Drive.

You can communicate much better with your dog once you know how to enhance certain Drives in him. However, sometimes your dog will be in the wrong Drive for a particular training session. Knowing how to direct him towards the correct Drive will be very helpful. If your dog is in Pack Drive and you need to switch to Prey Drive, just look at the previous list and follow the rules. Your dog should be able to switch into the desired Drive in no time.

Eliciting Defense Drive.

On the other hand, if your dog is in Prey Drive and he needs to be in Pack Drive, you must first put him into Defense Drive. Prey Drive is very stimulating (active), and dogs need to be brought back into neutral before being effectively put into Pack Drive. Pack is an orderly Drive because pack order is part of that Drive. Follow the rules for Defense Drive, then follow those for Pack Drive, and your dog should be able to move into Pack Drive from Prey Drive.

Practice switching your dog's Drives around and watch his responses in each. Notice that your dog's ears are pricked when he's in Prey Drive. Be aware that in Defense/ Flight Drive, they are back and down.

Dogs are most happy in the Drives that are high for them. Dogs are uncomfortable if they are in a Drive that is too low. Learn to read your dog, and you will learn to make your dog happy.

COUCH POTATO

This trick has more to it than meets the eye. First of all, being a true couch potato takes natural instinct and born talent. This is said with sarcasm, yet it has some validity. *The couch potato trick requires only low Drives—low Prey, Pack, Fight, and Flight.* This could be the trick of your dreams. However, being born with low Drives is a natural instinct. Not all dogs are born couch potatoes.

1   Get your dog.

2   Get the remote control.

3   Go to the couch. Lie down on one end.

4   Invite your dog to lie on the other end, with the command, "Let's do the Couch Potato trick."

This sounds silly, but the point is that all dogs do something naturally. Find what that natural thing is, label it, and then teach your dog to do it on command. If your dog gets on the couch without an invitation, teach him to get up there on command. If your dog lies under your desk while you sit at it, teach him to go there on command. If your dog begs for food when you eat popcorn in the living room, teach him to beg on command.

Look at your dog as a professional dog trainer would look at him. See what your dog does *naturally* that you would like him to do on command. Decide what you will call this trick, figure out the command, and then follow the steps, as in "Wagging Your Tail."

When you teach your dog something new, remember to praise him while he does the trick. When he's finished, release him and give him lots of rewards—whether it is hugs and kisses (Pack Drive)—or food treats (Prey Drive).

Chapter 2

What Every Good Trick Dog Should Know

Picture your dog sitting in the middle of a pile of dog treats on a Stay or quietly lying Down next to a coffee table laden with pizza boxes. Every houseguest will envy these behaviors. Or imagine your dog waiting for you at the opened gate to your yard, at the park, or in the back of your car with the door wide open. Your amazing dog will awe most passersby. And these are only a few of the things that you—and your dog—can accomplish by following this chapter.

STAY

To Stay means to not do anything and to get praised for not doing anything. In other words, to Stay is to hurry up and do nothing. This is an interesting concept for your dog.

Up until now you have been trying hard to get your dog to do something when you give her a command. With Stay, you are instead trying to convey, "When you do *nothing*, you are such a good dog." At first your dog may think that you are crazy to praise her for nothing. That is why your dog actually has to NOT stay to *learn* STAY. Saying nothing and putting your dog back into position when she does not Stay will teach her what Stay means.

The sitting position is probably the easiest way to teach the Stay because it is easy to put your dog back into a sitting position by simply lifting the leash over your dog's head and repositioning the dog into the Sit.

Sequence 1. Introduce your dog to the Stay command.

1 On leash, place your dog into a sitting position and praise her for sitting. If you need to help your dog to sit, tuck your arm behind her rear legs and fold her back legs up while gently lifting her collar. Give her lots of praise.

Show your dog the hand signal
for Stay and say, "Stay."

2   Tell your dog to "Stay," and give a hand signal for Stay. Use any signal you choose. The most commonly used hand signal is showing the palm of your hand with the fingers pointing down. During this first step, help your dog by gently holding the leash slightly taut over her head.

3   If your dog moves, say nothing and reposition the Sit. Smile, KNOWING that your dog needs to NOT stay in order to learn the Stay.

4   Relax the leash pressure, praise, and say, "OK."
After saying OK, run forward with your dog to show her that this really is the release and that now it's okay to move. There needs to be a clear difference between "Stay" and the release word that allows the dog to move.

Sequence 2. It's time to give your dog a little responsibility.

1   Sit your dog. Say, "Stay," and show her your hand signal.

2   Keep your hands near your waist with no pressure on the dog's leash. Remain close to your dog, holding the leash with nothing swinging loose. Remember that this is too stimulating for a high Prey Drive dog. Step in front of your dog this time with the leash in your hand and no pressure over your dog's head.

3   Step back to the side of your dog and praise her. Your dog should remain in the Stay while she is verbally praised. Your dog should remain in the Stay until you give the release word and run forward with her.

4   During the Stay, try to walk all the way around your dog. Walk near your dog as you walk around. Gently place your hand on her head as you circle once around. This first time, your dog will probably try to follow you as you go around. If this happens, just gently put your dog back into a sitting position and continue around.

5   If your dog moves from position, take the leash close to the collar and pull it up over your dog's head. If necessary, tuck your dog's rear legs back into a Sit. Say nothing until your dog is sitting still again, then smile and praise her. Don't forget that your dog needs a big release word to signal it's okay to move. Silently keep repeating the sitting position, even if your dog stands up, lies Down, or follows you. Remember, this is helping to convey the message that you want your dog to do NOTHING. Give her a big "OK" release, and then run forward *with* your dog after you say the release word.

Sequence 3. Gradually increase the time that you expect your dog to Sit and Stay.

1   Sit your dog. Say, "Stay," and then step out in front of your dog.

2   Remain in front of your dog for 10 seconds at a time. *Gradually* work up to five minutes.

3   As long as you give your dog lots of praise and a clear release word (OK), the Stay will become easier and easier. Your dog is not wrong for moving, so don't say anything; just put her back into a Sit. Teach your dog to sit still until she's released.

4   Remember that your dog has to NOT Stay and has to be PUT BACK into position in order to learn the Stay.

Sequence 4. Distance

1   Once the length of time has been increased successfully, you start moving away from your dog a few feet at a time. Start with three feet on leash.

Your dog should stay until she is given the release word, "OK."

2   If three feet is successful, move to six feet on leash the next time.

3   Eventually take the leash off and practice putting your dog back into a sitting position *without* the use of the leash. If your dog gets up, slowly go back to the dog and tuck her into a Sit using the collar and a little rear leg tuck if necessary.

4   Remain at six feet off leash until your dog is really solid on the command Stay. Also, your dog will need practice being put back without using the leash. This way, when you get to greater distances, your dog will not leave as you approach to put her back into the sitting position.

5   Move farther and farther away, increasing your distance two feet at a time.

Sequence 5. Distractions

Take your dog to a shopping center and practice while people go in and out.

1   After you can do a six-foot Sit-Stay with no leash for five minutes, it is time to start doing Stays around distractions. Take your dog to the corner store and practice out front while people are walking in and out.

2   Go to the park during a sports event.

3   Hold your own sports event and throw balls and toys around while your dog is on the Stay.

4   Remember, each time your dog moves from position, silently go back and reposition the Sit. The slower you move around your dog on a Sit-Stay, the more chance you have for success. *Remember the Prey Drive is stimulated by lots of motion.* Your arms, your hair, your necktie, or your leash can all swing too much and make it difficult for your dog to Stay. Help your dog to be successful!

THE STAY TRICK CHALLENGE

Here is where the Stays really become FUN. *Stays are Pack Drive behaviors.* When you add the challenge, you test your dog's knowledge of the Stay command. When you use a Prey Drive challenge: food, toys, or movement, you stimulate your dog's Prey Drive.

Be ready for what may happen. Your dog might move on the Stay command. You will need to react immediately, but remember to move *slowly* around your dog. Don't use a Defensive challenge such as a loud noise. It isn't fair, and if your dog has much Flight Drive, it will cause her too much stress. You can even use a Pack Drive challenge. Have someone come up and talk to or even pet your dog while she's on the Stay command. If your dog is high in Pack Drive, you might get lots of tail wagging or even a jump up. Be ready to put your dog back into position. Have fun with this.

Challenge your dog on the Stay:

1 Give the "Stay" command and toss a piece of food on the ground in front of your dog. Remember, your dog must Stay or be put back.

2 Make sure *you* (not the dog) get the food if the Stay is broken when the dog lunges for the food.

3 Reset the Stay position, say nothing, and throw the food again.

4 If you see no movement when the food is tossed, signal the release and let your dog eat the food. *This is a real challenge. Don't try this until you have done all the preliminary work leading up to it.* To be fair to your dog, she needs to understand the word "Stay" before you try the food challenge. Have fun with the Stay command. It can be a trick in itself.

Challenge your dog on Stays once she understands the command.

5 Ask a bystander, "Can you do something distracting so I can see if my dog breaks the Stay?" Be fair and work up to big distractions like kids, bikes, or Frisbees. Practice makes perfect!

6 Always remember to give a big release and let your dog eat the distraction—if possible—or play with a toy reward in its place. Always give lots of love with your releases.

LEADERSHIP EXERCISES

Respect is very important when you work with your dog. You must respect your dog, and your dog must respect you. Your responsibility lies in treating your dog with fairness and kindness.

Learning something new can be very confusing at first, before your dog "gets it." Until then, take everything *step by step.* Show your dog exactly what you want and praise her lavishly even though *you* did all of the work. You placed, moved, and then helped the dog and *she* gets all the glory. Praise and clap your hands, cheer with glee, and give her a treat when she does well or tries hard. Dogs love training sessions and the time you spend together. Your dog will start to try harder and harder to beat you to the punch. Before long, she'll do all the work, and *you* can sit back and take in all the applause.

Your dog's responsibility, as far as respect goes, is to learn to work *for you.* *The difference between working for someone and working with someone is simple: The leader makes up the rules of the game.* You decide when you are going to play and for how long. You own the ball, and you are going to let your dog play with it—but it's *your game.* You will play fair, and you will have fun, but, simply said, *you* are the coach, and your dog is the player. As I said before, respect works both ways—from you to your dog and from your dog to you. If you have ever been coached, you know that you work a lot harder for someone you respect than for someone you don't.

The best way to teach your dog leadership is to do a simple sequence of exercises called the Long Sit and the Long Down. These exercises are very easy. All you need is your dog, a timepiece, and a smile. Let's start with the Long Down.

THE LONG DOWN

Sequence 1. This should be done three times before going to Sequence 2.

1   Sit on the floor and place your dog into a Down position next to you. Praise quietly, but do not release your dog from the Down position. Keep your hands off during this exercise *except* to put the dog back into a Down position.

2   Start timing for 30 minutes. Try not to panic (see the note at the end of the list). It is a good idea to use a half-hour sitcom to keep some levity in your attitude.

3   Every time your dog gets up, put her
    back into the Down position. Take
    your hands off once your dog is
    Down, even if only for a few
    seconds.

4   If your dog pushes against you,
    move away slightly. Stay on
    the floor nearby so that you
    are close enough to put her
    back Down immediately.

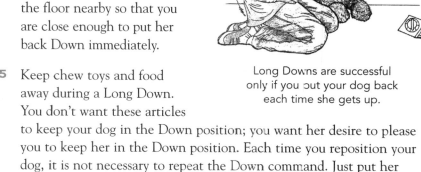

Long Downs are successful
only if you put your dog back
each time she gets up.

5   Keep chew toys and food
    away during a Long Down.
    You don't want these articles
    to keep your dog in the Down position; you want her desire to please
    you to keep her in the Down position. Each time you reposition your
    dog, it is not necessary to repeat the Down command. Just put her
    back. Smile to yourself—you know what a great learning opportunity
    this is!

6   After 30 minutes, praise and give your dog a BIG RELEASE. Say,
    "OK," and make her get up and move. If she fell asleep, wake her
    up for the release.

7   Do this three times during the next few days.

Important Note: To be successful at this leadership exercise, your dog
does not need to be perfectly still while she's in the Down position for the full
30 minutes. But to be successful, *every time your dog gets up, she needs to be put
back into the Down position.* This will create a *successful* training session. You
can do it—you just need to clearly tell your dog what you want—and what you
want is that she remain next to you in a Down position for the determined
amount of time.

Sequence 2. This step should be done three times before moving to Sequence 3.

1   Sit in a chair next to your dog in the Down position. This elevates
    your posture and distances you slightly from the dog. It shows that
    you can maintain control from a chair a few inches away.

Elevate your position
by sitting in a chair.

2   Time this Long Down for 30 minutes also, and then release your dog after the time is up. The same rules apply as in Sequence 1; always put your dog back into the Down if she should move or get up.

3   It is advisable to distract yourself during these sessions. You might want to watch a half-hour TV show. When the show starts, Down your dog. When the show ends, release your dog. TV can also help you pass the time. But don't get so distracted that you forget about your number one player, your dog. Keep an eye out so that you can reposition your dog when necessary.

4   Do this three times over the course of a few days. On alternate days do the Long Sit. (See "The Long Sit" later in this chapter.)

Sequence 3. Follow the same steps seen in Sequence 2, except that now you are in a chair a few feet away.

1   Put your dog in a Down position and then go sit down yourself.

2   As before, get up and reposition your dog into the Down position if she should move.

3   Increase the distance between you and your dog to 8–10 feet over the next three sessions.

4   Release your dog after 30 minutes.

5   Practice this sequence three times, alternating with the Long Sit.

Sequence 4. This should be done at least three times and repeated any time you need a little extra control in your relationship with your dog.

1   As in Sequence 3, after your dog is in a Down position, sit in a chair.

2   But don't stay in your chair the entire time. Move around the room occasionally. Get up and change the channel on the TV or go look out the window. Stand up and move to another chair. However, don't leave your dog's field of vision.

3   After 30 minutes, give the release and get your dog up with a big "OK."

4   Do Step 3 three times. Repeat as needed if the dog gets too keyed up.

THE LONG SIT

The Long Sit is the same as the Long Down, except that your dog is in a sitting position, and it is only done for 10 minutes. The Sit is a little less comfortable, so it is done for a shorter time period. Follow the different levels as for the Down.

Dogs who have had no trouble remaining in a Down will probably lie down during the Long Sit. This will give you the opportunity of reinforcing the Sit by showing your dog that you make the decisions. This is part of the exercise. You always *need* to reinforce the position if your dog moves.

1   Start with a 10-minute session with you in a chair next to your sitting dog. Do this three times on alternating days with the Long Down.

2   The next step is to do a 10-minute session while you are a short distance away from your sitting dog. Do this three times on alternating days with the Long Down.

3   Finally, do a 10-minute Sit while you move around the room in full view of your dog. Do this three times on days alternating with the Long Down.

Remember that the success of these exercises lies in the length of time they are done and in the fact that you always replace your dog when she gets up or changes position. Either the Long Sit or the Long Down will be more challenging for your dog. Spend more time on the one that requires more of your participation. Don't forget that the act of putting your dog *back* is the leadership element in these exercises. It is time well spent. Ten-minute Sits and 30-minute Downs are similar to the coach telling the track team to do 50 push-ups and then run 20 laps around the gym.

TAKE ME OUT TO THE BALL GAME: THE RETRIEVE

If your dog is a natural retriever, you are in luck. But not all dogs instinctively carry things in their mouths. Even if they do, they may not always want to give you those things. Chasing a moving article through the air doesn't light up every dog's life. *A dog with low Prey Drive will be harder to motivate towards retrieving than a dog with high Prey Drive.* A dog with high Prey *and* Pack Drives will not only want to go get the toy but will want to bring it *back to you also.*

You can get your dog to retrieve *anything!*

Wherever your dog falls on the Prey Drive scale, she can be taught to retrieve. It may take her a little longer, but with the help of some alternative methods, it can—and should—be done. A lot of tricks require dogs to hold something in their mouths. Even if your dog doesn't have to go get an item, holding it is an essential part of retrieving.

Let's Look at Each Part

1 **Chase** the item.

2 **Pick** it up.

3 **Hold** the item.

4 **Carry** it.

5 **Come back** to you with the item.

6 **Give it back** when you ask for it.

Where to Start

The Volhard Motivational Retrieve is a step-by-step approach that will create a solid retriever. Pick something that you want your dog to fetch—a stick, a ball, a dumbbell—even a piece of old leather.

1   Get some **treats** and offer one to your dog, saying "Take it" as she takes the treat from your fingers. You can offer the food on a spoon to help associate metal with retrieving. This will assist you if you ever want your dog to pick up something metal, like car keys or dropped silverware. Tell your dog "Take it" 10 times, and then stop. Do this again 10 times until your dog's mouth opens anxiously when you say, "Take it."

2   **Select something** for your dog to retrieve. As an example, I will use a stick. Hold a stick in one hand and gently open your dog's mouth with the other hand by putting your finger behind her canine tooth.

   Say, "Take it!" Gently place the stick in your dog's mouth and cup her mouth shut for two seconds while you smile and praise her. Exchange the stick for a treat while you say, "Give." Pet your dog between these attempts. Do this step 10 times and then take a break. Go for a short walk or play something else for a minute or so, and then do it 10 times

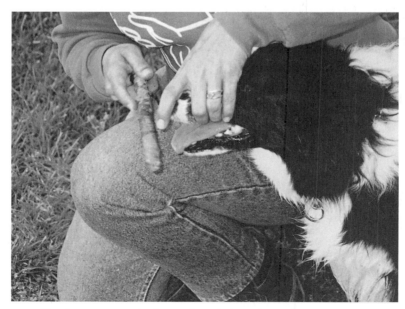

Gently open your dog's mouth and place the stick into position.

more. Do this step five times until your dog willingly holds the stick for just a few seconds while you gently keep her mouth closed. Always exchange her stick for a treat.

3   **Say, "Take it!"** Offer the stick in front of your dog's nose, tickling her lip with it. Place your dog next to you on the left, holding her collar with two fingers of your left hand while you tickle her nose with the stick in your right hand. If your dog takes the stick, let go of her collar and cup her mouth shut as you did in the last step. Then praise her and smile.

After just a couple of seconds, exchange the stick for a treat. If your dog shows any sign of taking the stick, place it in your dog's mouth and cup her mouth shut. Praise your dog and then exchange the stick for food with the "Give" command. Some signs that your dog wants to retrieve are:

- Staring at the stick
- Licking her nose or lips
- Bumping the stick with her nose

If you see any of these signs, place the stick in your dog's mouth as if she had taken it herself. Do this step only as long as it takes for your dog to voluntarily take the stick.

Cup your dog's mouth shut after positioning the stick.

4   Once your dog willingly takes the stick, you need to teach her to hold it. Go back to placing it in the dog's mouth and cupping her mouth shut. Praise her. Slowly bring your hand under your dog's mouth and help lift her muzzle into a natural position for carrying the stick.

Smile and praise—it means a lot to your dog to see you smile. Tell your dog "Hold it." Lower your hand slightly and repeat "Hold it." Gently lift the muzzle again if the dog starts to roll the stick around in her mouth or isn't holding it firmly. Say, "Hold it." After just five seconds the first time, say, "Give," and remove the stick from her mouth. Remember to exchange it for a treat and give lots of praise between each hold.

Never let your dog drop the item into your hands or onto the floor. Work up to 30 seconds for holding it, five seconds at a time. If your dog drops the stick, be more enthusiastic about lifting her muzzle with a little tap under the jaw. *Remember your dog's Drives. With high Flight Drive, just lifting the muzzle will be enough.*

5   Reaching for the stick is the next step. With your dog on your left, slide two fingers into her collar. With your right hand about two inches in front of your dog's nose, offer

Teach your dog to hold the stick.

her the stick and say, "Take it." If your dog reaches for the stick, cup her mouth shut and pile on the praise. Exchange the stick for a food reward and do a happy dance.

If your dog doesn't offer to take the stick, keep it just in front of her nose. Move the stick with your dog's nose. As a correction, slightly twist the collar to tighten it a little. Hold the pressure for only a few seconds if your dog has much Flight Drive. *If she has plenty of Fight Drive, hold it for no more than 20 seconds.*

Watch for any signs that the dog is thinking about taking the stick, as you did earlier. If you see any sign at all, or think you do, relax the collar and put the stick into your dog's mouth. Praise *heavily* as though it was the dog's idea to take the stick.

After the pressure, put the stick in your dog's mouth even if she didn't take it.

Gently lift your dog's muzzle if she stops having a firm grip on the stick.

Exchange the stick for food and try again. Keep trying until your dog truly does take the stick. The key here is to make the exchange lots of fun using nothing more than smiles and praise. Your dog needs to enjoy training sessions and so do you. Take breaks after every few repetitions.

6   Once your dog holds the stick and reaches for it alone, you need to teach her to hold the stick while walking. Place the stick in your dog's

Teach your dog to walk while she holds the stick.

mouth, say, "Hold it" and "Let's go." Gently help your dog to walk as you lift her muzzle up into a natural position. Take only a few steps at a time and then exchange the stick for food. If your dog drops the stick, just stop and do a 30 second stick hold right where you are. Try to get your dog to walk while she holds the stick. Lots of praise and enthusiasm will teach your dog that she is doing the right thing. Remember, *lots and lots* of praise.

7   Once your dog can walk while holding the stick, you are just one step away from true retrieving. Your dog must be able to pick up the stick from the ground. Try to get your dog to take the stick while walking. Keep the stick just a few inches in front of her nose.

     Move with your dog and present the stick just in front of her for a moving retrieve. Move along with your dog and say, "Take it." After each moving retrieve, exchange the stick for food and then praise your dog. Gradually lower the stick as you move along. Get your dog to lower her head and grab for the stick. Give lots of praise and make it as much fun as you can. Finally, put one end of the stick on the floor and hold the other end up on an angle. Tell your dog to take it. Wow! Again, give her *lots of praise.* If your dog needs to be reminded, use a little collar pressure to move her toward the stick and help her pick it up. *The more help your dog needs, the more praise she should get.*

     If your dog loses interest, you have either played too long or haven't made retrieving enough fun for your dog. *Remember her Drives.* Lots of activity is fun for dogs with lots of Prey Drive. Lots of petting, smiles, and hugs is fun for dogs with lots of Pack Drive. Make the stick the prize for dogs with lots of Fight Drive. *You just need to know what motivates your dog and then utilize it.*

Your dog must be able to pick the stick up from the ground.

8   Once your dog picks up the object from the ground, you are ready.

Throw the stick and send your dog after it at the same time. This is called a *live retrieve,* and it is usually very motivating. Call your dog back to you as soon as she picks up the stick. After this becomes routine, you won't need to actually call the dog during a retrieve. The dog should automatically bring the item back to you.

Make sure to reward your dog for each retrieve. With some dogs, just throwing the toy again is their reward. Others will require something more.

9   Finally, you can put the Stay (see Page 15) together with the Retrieve. Your dog should not go after something you have thrown until you tell her to get it.

If you have practiced the Stay Challenge, this will be very easy. Tell your dog to Stay and then throw a toy. Wait a second and then tell your dog to "Take it." After all of your training, your dog should fly out to the item, pick it up, and bring it directly back to you. What a good dog! If all does not go as planned, it is time for a little review, and that is okay.

It is never a problem to review your training. It's all part of working and playing with a dog. Remember, repetition—along with fun and consistency—is part of the whole picture. Keep up the good work.

Chapter 3

Practical Tricks

Tricks range in category from entertaining to handy. Here are some practical, useful tricks that will not only impress your friends but might also aid you in your daily tasks and in "living with" your dog.

DOOR MANNERS (THE INVISIBLE DOOR)

Having a dog with door manners may be your best trick yet. The trick is teaching your dog to never cross a threshold without permission. Some examples of thresholds (invisible doors) are the front door, the back door, the gate to your fenced yard, the car door, the basement door, and the top of the stairs. The list can be endless.

Not only will this trick amaze people, it will also be the most practical thing that you teach your dog. Imagine someone leaving the gate to your back yard ajar and your dog staying in the yard. Imagine your dog never trying to run out the front door unattended or staying in the car while you load and unload the parcels that you are carrying. Imagine your dog waiting at the top of the stairs instead of getting underfoot and tripping you.

It really is simple. With just a few training sessions you will be wondering how you *ever* lived with a dog who didn't have door manners.

Pack Drive is necessary here because it requires maximum cooperation from your dog. Some Defense/Fight Drive is also helpful for this trick. Make this trick enjoyable with lots of *fun releases*, and it will be possible for almost any dog.

Sequence 1. Put your dog on leash for a training session at the front door of your house or apartment.

The commands you will use are: "Wait" and "OK." "*Wait*" will signal your dog *not to cross* the threshold. "OK" will signal permission to cross the threshold. Obviously, you will not always use "OK" because sometimes your dog will not be leaving with you. At those times, you are free to leave home without your dog following at your heels or bolting out the door.

Start by walking up to the door with your dog on leash. Open the door. Make sure your dog's leash is loose and that you are not pulling or holding him back. Open the door as you say, "Wait." The instant your dog starts to cross the threshold, quickly pull on his leash to bring him back in. Close the door and try again. Act as if you had nothing to do with your dog's being pulled back into the room. There you are just smiling and saying, "What a good dog!" Your dog thinks, "Hmm, it must have been the *threshold* that pulled me back. My *owner* is fine and happy. I think I'll stay on this side of the door with my owner." Remember:

1   **Open** the door with your dog on a **loose** leash.

2   **Say, "Wait."**

3   **Pull back** quickly on the leash if the dog's foot starts to cross the threshold.

4   Let the **door close** with both of you still inside.

After waiting at the threshold for a few seconds, say, "Okay," and then let your dog cross over with you.

5   **Act** as if you had nothing to do with the pull back. Praise your dog.

6   **Repeat** until your dog starts to hesitate crossing the threshold.

Sequence 2. Repeat Step 1, but instead of closing the door, hesitate and say, "OK" and let your dog cross over the threshold.

This should help make it clear for the dog not to move until permission is given.

1   **Open** the door and **say**, "Wait."

2   **Pull back** if your dog should start to cross.

3   **Say, "OK,"** and let your dog cross.

From here on, you can never allow your dog to go through the front door without you saying, "OK," even when you are just going for a walk *with* your dog. You need to be consistent. Remind yourself with a note taped to the door frame. Simply say, "OK" *when* you and your dog go outside *together*.

To reinforce your leadership, it's a good idea that you cross all thresholds first. Just remember that your dog is being taught never to cross any threshold without hearing "OK." You want—and need—to be consistent so that your dog understands. To be clear and fair to your dog, be consistent.

Sequence 3. This time *you* are going through the door and the dog *is not*.

Remember, always approach the door with a loose leash—don't *hold* your dog back. If your dog tries to cross, quickly pull him back.

Next, you need to step just out-side and pull the leash back into the house if your dog tries to follow. You will do this by extending your arm back into the doorway and pulling the leash around the door. Open the door and be ready to pull the leash back in the house if your dog tries to join you on the outside. Then say, "OK" and let your dog join you with lots of praise.

While you are on the other side of the threshold from your dog, reach back in to put your dog back if he starts to cross over.

1   **Open** the door with your dog on a loose leash.

2   **Say, "Wait."**

3   **Pull back** on the leash before the dog's foot crosses the opening.

4   **Go out**, but extend your arm through the door, pulling back if your dog follows. **Let the door close** on the leash.

5   **Open** the door and keep your dog from coming out toward you.

6   **Say, "OK"** and let your dog come to you.

7   Give lots and lots of praise.

Sequence 4. Do Sequences 1 through 3 coming *back into* the house.

Sequence 5. Take the leash off.

Walk up to the door with your dog and say, "Wait." When you open the door, be ready to pull the door back quickly if your dog's nose starts to poke out. Don't actually close the door on his nose, just make it come closer to create an impression on your dog. Start to open the door again, close the door quickly, and pull back on your dog's collar to remind him not to cross. Then open the door and go through yourself. Keeping the door open, look back at your dog and say, "OK." Then let him come with you, giving him lots of praise.

1   **Open** the door with your dog off leash.

2   **Say, "Wait."**

3   **Before** the dog's foot crosses the opening, **pull back quickly** on the door and/or the dog's collar.

4   **Open the door** and go out alone.

5   **Say, "OK"** and welcome your dog through.

Sequence 6. Start all over with other doors and exits.

Start with Sequence 1 at the backyard gate and go all the way through Sequence 5. Then start with Sequence 1 again for your car doors and go all the way through Sequence 5. Practice at any door, threshold, or exit that your dog should not cross without permission.

Sequence 7. If you have more than one dog, train one dog at a time so each has his own opportunity to learn door manners.

After all your dogs have learned and mastered door manners, you should be able to handle the group at the door with no leashes. Allow only the dog you call to cross the threshold to be with you.

Nothing will impress your friends more when they come to visit. But keep in mind, practice makes perfect.

GO AHEAD, MAKE MY DAY

You can even teach your dog not to cross a chalk line on the floor or in the dirt in the same manner. Just draw the line and take your dog through Sequences 1 through 5, using the line as a threshold. You can teach your dog just about anything.

You can re-enact old western movies. Draw the line on the floor and say, "OK, go ahead. I dare you to cross this line." Your dog will cross over because you said, "OK." Then look nervously at your dog and draw another line. Say, "Well, how about this line? Go ahead, OK, go ahead." Then do it *one more time* and really start to sweat. Draw a line and say, "I dare you to cross THIS line. Go ahead, what's stopping you? OK." When your dog crosses it, run for the hills, and get your *dog* to *chase you.* You should win an Academy Award for this sequence.

STAIR MANNERS

How many times have you competed with your dog for right of way on the stairs? This can be very dangerous for both you and your dog—not to mention guests. Teaching your dog that going up and down the stairs as a solo act as not only wise, it is safety rule number two. Door manners are safety rule number one.

Just as with doors, set up training sessions on the stairs in your house. With your dog on leash, approach the top of the stairs and say, "Wait." Then start down the steps. If your dog follows, pull back on the leash to place him back at the top of the stairs. Start down the stairs again. If the stairs are long, leave the leash draped over the steps. *Go back, take the leash, and begin again if your dog follows you.* Stair Masters have nothing on stair manners. You may be going back up the stairs each time you get to the bottom if your dog follows you before you have said, "OK." When you finally get to the bottom, turn, face your dog, and say, "OK." *Remember to give your dog lots of praise when he gets to you.*

Teach door manners before stair manners so your dog understands what "Wait" means, unless you want the exercise running up and down the stairs to begin again when your dog follows you.

CLEAN UP YOUR ROOM
OR PICK UP YOUR LAUNDRY

Everybody in your household should be responsible for his or her own mess and should clean it up willingly. Some of us have more chores than others do, but even the smallest members of the family need to pull their own weight.

Your dog is no different. He gets free room and board—of course your dog should pick up his own toys! This may mean that you need to buy your dog a lot of new toys and an appropriate toy chest. I don't think you will get any objections from your dog on this point.

Prey Drive is what makes dogs want to play with most toys, especially squeaky toys and flying, floppy toys. Soft cloth toys can be Prey Drive toys too, unless your dog mothers them. In that case, they are Pack Drive toys. Make sure you get your dog's favorite type of toy so that playing with them is fun for both of you. Your dog's toy chest should be the appropriate size for him to drop his toys into.

1   You will need to teach your dog to **retrieve** with the sequences in "Take Me Out to the Ball Game: The Retrieve" (see Page 24). You need to have a reliable *fetch command* in order for your dog to pick up all the toys and ultimately put them all away. After you have mastered the "Take It" command, and your dog brings the wanted items to you, you are ready to move on.

2   Next, teach your dog to pick up different things from around the room—on *your command*. The steps for teaching this are in the trick "Find What I Have Lost" (Page 45). If your dog's ball is in the middle of the living room floor when you point to it and say, "Take your ball," will your dog bring it to you? If not, work on getting your dog to retrieve different toys for you as you take them, and then ask for another toy. Label the toys by name as in "Find What I Have Lost." Remember to reward your dog for each toy he brings you. In the retrieving tricks, throwing the item again is part of the reward.

With this trick, the item is not thrown again. Therefore, you must praise your dog adequately when he gives the item to you. During the learning process, *use each toy* and play with your dog for a few minutes before you ask for another toy. Put each toy away and then ask for another. This will be more fun for your dog than when he immediately gives up each item.

With your dog's free room and board comes picking up his toys.

Start with a pile of toys on the floor. Ask your dog to bring you a toy. Play with it for a few seconds and then say, "Give." Take the toy, release your dog, and hand him a treat. Put the toy in the box yourself, and then ask him to bring you another toy. Point to the pile and request the next toy. Repeat this process until all the toys have been brought to you and have been put away.

End the training session by playing with a favorite toy and permitting your dog to keep it. If you ask for the toys, put them away, and then ignore the dog when he has no toys, your dog will quickly learn not to participate in this trick. Why should he? He ends up with no toys and no fun! So, as always, try to look at the trick from your dog's point of view. He needs to see that bringing all the toys, one by one, will end with him getting to keep the best one—and getting to play with the rest of them along the way.

3   Now it is time to teach your dog to "Drop" the toys into the box rather than to "Give" them to you. Gather up some toys and get the toy box yourself.

Give your dog a toy rather than having him pick one up. This way, you are working on pieces of the trick one at a time. First, you will drop the toy into the box. Therefore, *do not* work on retrieving or identifying. Have the toy box right next to you and tell your dog to "Put it away." Offer your hand over the box, and if your dog drops the toy, move your hand and let the toy go directly into the box. Give your dog lots of praise. Reward him either with a treat or by letting him play with the put-away toy.

If your dog doesn't offer you the toy, gently remove it by opening your dog's mouth with mild pressure above the lips over his teeth. If you press lightly with your dog's lips over the upper teeth, his mouth should open. Give him tremendous praise for dropping the item into the box. Toss it out of the box and let your dog play with it again as a reward. Stop after you have had any amount of success with this. You should always end each training session on a fun note.

4   Practice the "Put it away" command daily. Offer your dog a toy right next to the box. Say, "Put it away." Help him drop it into the box with lots of praise and play. Make dropping the toy into the box the game. The easier it is for your dog, the more fun it becomes because you are making training into a game.

Work on this trick until your dog no longer needs your help to drop the toy into the box. You will be ready to put all the steps together once you can offer your dog a toy from a few feet away from the box, command "Put it away," and watch as he walks to the box and drops in the toy.

5   Combine Step 2 and Step 4. Have a couple of toys near the box. Ask your dog to "Get" a particular toy. Now tell your dog to "Put it away." Help guide your dog to the box. Tap the edge of the box and point into it. Remember to help your dog when necessary. When the toy is in the box, praise your dog and give him the release word *and* a treat. This is not only great fun for your dog, but it will help you too.

6   Now you are ready for your dog to do the pick-up chores. Scatter several toys around the room. Place the toy box in an easily accessible spot in the same room. Command your dog to "Get" a toy, and then command your dog to "Put it away." At this point, it should not be necessary to help, but it is better to review than to get frustrated if your dog is having trouble. Training is all about having *patience*.

You can teach your dog to pick up any item that he is trained to retrieve. Use your imagination to impress houseguests with this trick. You can practice using cloth napkins at the coffee table. Keep a laundry basket nearby and have your dog help you clean up after the guests have finished eating. Or use paper napkins and have your dog throw them in the trash basket. If your guests have taken their shoes off, have your dog place them in the shoe basket. Remember, let your imagination be your limitation.

GO FIND DADDY *OR* WAKE UP THE KIDS *OR* TAKE THIS TO GRANDMA

You can save your legs—and your mind—by sending your dog through the house to help you find a family member. Waking up the kids in the morning can be a breeze if you enlist the help of the family dog. If you have a four-footed friend, finding a lost hobbyist in the bowels of the basement or attic is no longer impossible. And waiting on guests is far more entertaining when you have someone with floppy ears helping out. So why do it alone? Teach your dog to become your sidekick for all of these daily tasks.

Dogs can carry notes or requests in their mouths. They can jump up on beds to awaken impossible sleepers. Dogs can even transport items—tied to their collars like a butler with a tray—to the far reaches of your house.

With a few simple steps, this practical and fun trick can be made into one of the best uses for your dog's abilities. After all, everyone deserves to earn his keep. This trick has elements of Pack, Prey, and Defense Drive in it. Pack Drive comes from finding another pack member, Prey Drive is in running and carrying, and Defense/Fight Drive is in having the confidence to leave the room alone.

1   Start with one other person in the household. Decide on the names that your dog will know you by. For example, when your dogs *are* the kids in the family, the adults can be Mommy and Daddy. So the commands can be "Go find Daddy" and "Go find Mommy." When there are more than two people in the household, proper names can be used, but start teaching this trick with just two of you. Your dog first needs to learn to find *one other* person *before* he can discriminate between different people in the house.

2   Get your dog, some treats, the person to be found, and a long leash or line.

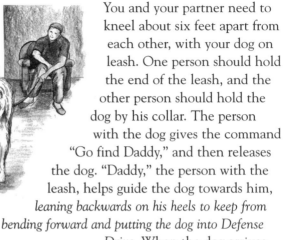

You and your partner need to kneel about six feet apart from each other, with your dog on leash. One person should hold the end of the leash, and the other person should hold the dog by his collar. The person with the dog gives the command "Go find Daddy," and then releases the dog. "Daddy," the person with the leash, helps guide the dog towards him, *leaning backwards on his heels to keep from bending forward and putting the dog into Defense Drive.* When the dog arrives, "Daddy" offers a small treat, taking the dog gently by the collar and praising him.

Increase the distance between two people until they are in different rooms.

"Daddy" should make the experience very pleasant and fun for the dog. After all, your dog has found "Daddy"—and that's wonderful.

While "Daddy" is praising the dog, he should toss the end of the leash back to you. Do this back and forth several times, the full length of the leash, until your dog is flying between the two of you, always waiting for the command, "Go find so and so." Change the length of time between commands. By making the times random between calls, you will be teaching your dog to learn the command, "Go find someone," rather than teaching him just to run back and forth between the two of you.

To Recap

Have your dog on leash.
Two people kneel, facing each other the same distance apart as the leash is long.
One person holds the leash; the other holds the dog.
The person with the dog says, "Go find so and so."
The leash holder helps guide the dog to him or her.
The same person holds the collar, feeds the dog, and praises him.
Switch roles with your partner.

3   Take the leash off and increase the distance between the two people
    by only a few feet. Repeat as in Step 2, but this time, *don't use the
    leash.* If your dog doesn't go to your partner directly, then it is your job
    to silently take the dog's collar and walk him to the indicated person.
    When your dog gets there, even if with human assistance, the "found
    person" should really lay on the praise. Make your dog want to find
    that person the next time.

    If your dog needs help too many times in a row, simply put his
    leash back on and continue with Step 2. If you are successful, gradual-
    ly increase the distance between both people. Try to stay in sight of
    each other. Remember to hold your dog until you send him, and then
    help your dog (if necessary) without giving another command.

To Recap

Have your dog off leash.
Two people kneel, facing each other a short distance apart.
One person holds the dog.
The person with the dog says, "Go find so and so," and lets go of the
    dog. When the dog finds the person indicated, that person takes
    hold of the collar, feeds the dog, and praises him.
If the dog doesn't go, the sender should take him to the hunted person.
    Praise the dog just the same.
Switch roles.

4   Now that your dog is doing his finding without a leash, gradually move
    out of sight of one another. First go just around the corner, and then go
    to another room down the hall. Eventually, go upstairs and downstairs.

    It is very important to change the length of time between com-
    mands. You want your dog to perform *on command*, not to just run
    between the two of you, grabbing the treat, and then running back
    again. Take hold of your dog's collar and praise him with a treat reward.
    Then wait and send your dog back on command.

To Recap

Have your dog off leash.
Two people kneel out of sight of one another.
The person with the dog says, "Go find so and so," and lets the dog go.
When the dog finds the person indicated, that person takes hold of the
     dog's collar and feeds and praises him.
If the dog doesn't go, the sender leads the dog to the hunted person.
     Praise the dog just the same.
Reverse roles.

5   At the beginning of each training session, go back to the previous step
for review. Practice these steps until your dog has no trouble finding
you or your partner.

    After many training sessions, try sending your dog to find your
partner *without* a review step. Cue your partner about your plan and go
to another part of the house. After a few minutes, command your dog,
"Go find Daddy." Remember, be ready to help your dog, but don't repeat
your command over and over again. If your dog goes right to the job
at hand and finds your partner, make sure that the found person gives
lots of praise to your dog. He certainly deserves to be rewarded!

To Recap

Without a review, but with a plan, send your dog to find someone.
When your dog finds the person indicated, that person takes hold of his
     collar, feeds the dog, and praises him.
If the dog doesn't go, the sender takes the dog to the hunted person.
     Praise him just the same.

6   After much success with Step 5, it is time to teach your dog to tell the
difference between family members. Start with everybody in a circle
and repeat Step 2 by using the leash again. Toss the leash to Sally and
command, "Go find Sally." Let her praise and reward and then toss
the leash to someone else. She then commands, "Go find Mommy."

Continue until you have named everyone, and your dog is having a great time waiting for the "Go find so and so" command and then finding that particular person.

To Recap

Get into a circle of people with your dog on leash.
One person should hold the leash while another holds the dog.
The person with the dog says, "Go find so and so."
The leash holder helps guide the dog to her.
The same person holds the dog's collar, feeds, and praises him.
Continue until everyone is named. Give your dog lots of praise.

7   Spread out your circle and take your dog off leash. Continue as in Step 6, randomly sending your dog to all the members of your circle. The sender should quietly help the dog find the right person, if necessary.

Make sure that your body posture is not putting your dog into Defense Drive. This may happen if you're towering over your dog or dragging him by his leash. The found person should also look very welcoming—she should kneel back on her heels, and allow the dog to come quickly and happily.

To Recap

Get into a circle of people with your dog off leash.
The person with the dog says, "Go find so and so."
The found person takes hold of the dog's collar and feeds him.
Continue until everyone is named. Give lots of praise to your dog.

8   As in Step 4, go out of sight and into different rooms of the house until your dog can run through the house and *find all* family members participating in this training session. It is not necessary to have all members of the family work on this step every time you practice. But do review the previous step with your dog when you start up each training session.

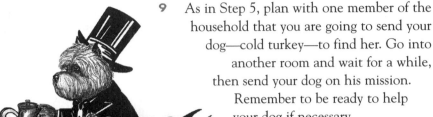

9 As in Step 5, plan with one member of the household that you are going to send your dog—cold turkey—to find her. Go into another room and wait for a while, then send your dog on his mission. Remember to be ready to help your dog if necessary.

These helping sessions are what make your desires clear to your dog. Don't ever lose your patience. Rather, quietly take your dog to the missing person. Even with your help, your dog should always get praised as if he's performing without any help.

When did you hire a butler?
Wait—isn't that Rover?!

To Recap

Without a review, but with a plan, send your dog to find someone.
When your dog finds the person indicated, that person takes hold of the collar, feeds the dog, and praises him a lot.
If your dog doesn't go, the sender should lead him back to the hunted person. Praise your dog just the same.

10 Use your imagination and figure out how to best use this trick. You could get a bell for your dog's collar to signal when he is carrying a note. Or try a doggie backpack when you want him to carry large items to other parts of the house. If your dog will hold something, then you can have him deliver the intended item to the lost family member.

NOTE: This trick is not recommended for sandwich delivery unless the other person is on a diet.

THE "LIVING VACUUM"

How many times have you dropped something while you were cooking? What do you do with food once it hits the floor? Certainly you can't use it. Plus, you have to bend over to pick it up. What you need is a vacuum cleaner that is available on an instant's notice, a vacuum that doesn't run out of battery power or require long cords. Sounds like a situation where your dog can come to the rescue, doesn't it? *Dogs with a fair amount of Prey Drive will do this trick naturally.* The vacuum trick is easy to teach.

1   Get several pieces of food. Start in the kitchen or in the eating area of your house. Casually drop a piece of food, point to it with your toe, and say, "Vacuum." Tap the floor with your toe *rather than* pointing with your finger. You want your dog to look down at the floor, not up at your hands. If necessary, place your hands out of sight as you tap the floor with your toe. Praise your dog when he finds the food and eats it. Release him with a big "OK."

2   Do not necessarily drop the bits of treat in full view of your dog. Distract your dog or have someone else distract him, drop something, and command, "Vacuum." When your dog automatically looks down upon hearing "Vacuum," you have successfully taught him the trick. Praise your dog while he looks for the tidbit. Release him after he eats it.

3   Reinforce this trick on a regular basis. Do not let too many days go by without practicing. If you are a clumsy chef or have kids who toss things at the table, your dog will be a pro in no time!

This trick teaches your dog to hunt for something on the floor using the "Vacuum" command. Have fun; your dog certainly will!

FIND WHAT I HAVE LOST

How many times a week do you hunt for misplaced keys—or worse—the remote control? Lost items can make you crazy. What better trick, then, could there be aside from teaching your dog to find your lost items? *A dog with a good nose for scent is essential for Prey Drive. Pack Drive involves finding the lost item and returning it. Because this trick uses both Drives, your dog will need some of each.*

1   First, you need to teach your dog to find something in particular and then bring it to you. Take your pick of items, but keep the following in mind: This is the training phase—you and your dog will be playing with this item, and it will spend a lot of time in your dog's mouth.

It's a good idea to start with keys because they are easy to wash. It might be even easier for your dog to pick up the keys if they are attached to a leather strap. Toss your keys around and see if your dog

will pick them up and carry them on the command, "Go find my keys." If he doesn't, refer back to the retrieving section (see Page 24) in this book.

2 After playing a retrieving game with your keys, play a game of "find" with them. While your dog is watching, toss your keys into a pile of pillows on the floor. Tell your dog, "Go find my keys." Help your dog look through the pillows if he seems confused. Really praise your dog for finding the keys even if you helped. Remember to treat your dog to a piece of his favorite food and release him with an "OK" after you take the keys from his mouth. Continue practicing this game of find in different locations and in piles of different items.

Toss your keys around and see if your dog will pick them up on command.

To Recap

Locate a pile of miscellaneous stuff.
Sit your dog nearby and let him watch as you toss the keys into the pile.
Send your dog with the command, "Go find my keys."
Help him if necessary.
Call your dog back when he has the keys in his mouth.
Praise, Release, Reward.

3 Repeat Step 2, BUT don't let your dog watch as you toss the keys into a pile. This is the "Secret Game of Find."

To Recap

Locate a pile of miscellaneous stuff.
Sit your dog facing away as you toss the keys into the pile.
Send your dog looking with the command, "Go find my keys."
Help if necessary.
Call your dog back with the keys in his mouth.
Praise, Release, Reward.

4 Repeat Step 3, except come upon the pile of stuff where you planted your keys earlier and ask your dog to, "Go find my keys." This is the "Surprise Game of Find."

To Recap

Plant your keys ahead of time in a pile of miscellaneous stuff.
Approach the pile with your dog.
Ask your dog to look for the article with the command, "Go find my keys."
Help if necessary.
Call your dog back with the keys in his mouth.
Praise, Release, Reward.

5 Repeat Step 4, but this time even you don't know where your keys are. This is called, "Help, Your Owner is a Scatterbrain!" Or "Lose Your Keys."

To Recap

Lose your keys.
Come upon your dog.
Ask your dog to look with the command, "Go find my keys."
Help if necessary, especially if you are running late.
Call your dog back with the keys in his mouth.
Praise, Release, Reward, and GO to Work!

6 This trick can be done with any commonly lost items. Practice by naming the items and teaching your dog these names. Start with something like your keys and the remote.

Play games of fetch with each item, *saying the name of the item in the game.* Then place both items out in front of your dog on a piece of rug

"Secret game of Find." You can help if necessary.

Tie different items to a peg board
and ask your dog to find the item
that isn't tied down.

or peg board. Tie one item to the rug or peg board with a string. Ask your dog to find the item that is not tied down. If your dog tries to get the wrong item, he won't be able to pick it up. You will not need to tell your dog "No" because he isn't doing anything wrong. He is getting something for you and is trying hard, so don't scold.

Just go up to your dog and point to the right item and praise him when he picks it up. Try again until the right one is repeatedly found. Trade on and off with each item by tying and untying them. After you have named different items for your dog, add them to the group by playing fetch with them. Then tie them to the rug or peg board. Do Steps 2 through 5 with each different item. The more you practice, the more your dog will know.

To Recap

Play fetch with the command, "Go find—whatever."
Start with two different items over the course of several sessions.
Tie one item to a rug or peg board.
Command your dog, "Go find whatever" for the untied item.
Help your dog, if necessary. Never reprimand him for trying to take the wrong thing. Go and point to the right item.
Alternate the items.
Add more items that you have named for your dog.
Do Steps 2 through 5 with each item.

7   Have friends over and place all of the potentially lost items into a box. Ask someone to hide an item while your dog is out of the room. Then bring your dog in and have him find it.

Don't allow your friends to be too creative with their hiding places. Remember, your dog is your best friend, and he doesn't want to make YOU look foolish.

PAPER ROUTE

So many times you hear people complain about what their dogs cost them. Yes, it's true that with dog food, veterinary visits, grooming fees, and toys, dogs are expensive. The best suggestion you can make to people who complain about costly canines is—*in good humor*—to suggest that their dog get a part-time job to help with expenses.

Find your dog a part time job!

One good idea is a paper route. The first house on the route should be the one where the dog lives. The paper should be delivered from the front porch or yard to the doorstep. A famous quote worthy of repeating here is, "Every journey begins with just one step." Updated it might be, "Every paper route begins with just one house." *Paper Delivery is truly a trick of Prey Drive. Your dog doesn't need to have much Prey, but a score better than 30 will make the trick a lot easier to teach. Coming back with the newspaper is part of Pack Drive—remember that any dog coming to you is exhibiting Pack behavior.*

1   Teach the retrieve using any object—a stick or a ball—it doesn't matter. See "Take Me Out to the Ball Game: The Retrieve" (Page 24). The command for this trick is "Take the paper."

2   Teach your dog to hold and carry the newspaper however it is delivered in your area. See "Take Me Out to the Ball Game: The Retrieve."

3   Put your dog on leash. It isn't safe for your dog to be out without a leash. Toss a paper near the delivery spot at your home. Tell your dog to "Take the paper." While your dog is going to get the paper, back up to the front door of your home. When your dog has the paper, call your dog to come to you. When he gets there, take the paper with the command, "Give." Praise with much enthusiasm and release by saying "OK." Remember to pay your paper boy for a job well done. (I think the going rate for paper delivery is a dog cookie a day.)

To Recap

Toss the paper.
Send your dog with the command, "Take the paper."
Back up to the door and call your dog to you.
Say, "Give."
Praise and Reward.

4   Preplant the newspaper and send your dog to look for it with the command, "Take the paper." After your dog has the paper, call him from the doorway and praise him. Say, "Give." Remember to give your dog a reward.

   If your dog needs help, go to the paper and point to it. *Don't repeat the command.* If he needs more help, take your dog to the paper and gently put it in his mouth. You are trying to make this fun, not scary. *You are not trying to put your dog into Defense/Flight Drive. Be careful.* If you help your dog by taking his collar, remain friendly and smiling. Don't allow your body posture to tower over your dog. Give him a lot of praise whether you helped him or not.

To Recap

Place the newspaper outside, but don't let your dog see you put it there.
Send your dog out with the command, "Take the paper."
Help him if necessary.
Call from the doorway with the word "Come."
Praise your dog for coming, and then say, "Give."
Praise him again and release.
Pay your delivery dog the going rate.
Practice makes perfect, and if any dog will make a living at this, you will
   need to practice. Have fun!

TUG OF WAR

Tricks can do more than entertain. They can also provide exercise and release pent-up energy.

   If you have a dog with lots of Prey Drive, what do you do with that dog? If you want to live peacefully with him, you need to use up all of his Prey

Drive. Otherwise, your dog will be walking on the ceiling. *Therefore, play lots of ball games and practice lots of retrieving with your dog to satisfy his Prey Drive.*

If you have a dog with lots of Pack Drive, what do you do with that dog? Most likely that dog follows you around the house all the time. *You pet and lavish love on Pack Drive dogs because they thrive on attention.* If you don't spend a lot of "Face Time" (hugs and kisses) with a high Pack Drive animal, he won't thrive and could

If you live with a Prey Drive–intense dog, you need to play lots of ball to survive.

become neurotic, causing him to bark uncontrollably or behave destructively.

So what do you do when your dog has an excess of Fight Drive? Most of the time, people try to squelch Fight Drive. They think they need to "keep a lid on it." But as you can see from the previous examples, if you don't give your dog adequate time in the appropriate Drives, problems arise. A dog with a lot of Fight Drive and no outlet might become a real problem. Fight Drive needs a place to go.

A good outlet for Fight Drive is controlled Tug of War games. Controlled means YOU make up the rules. Any dog can play Tug of War, but it can be particularly necessary for dogs with high Fight Drive.

Give your dog an outlet for Fight Drive.

Before starting any Tug of War games, if your dog has any Fight Drive at all, make sure that you have first done the Long Down and Long Sit exercises in order to establish the correct relationship (see Pages 20 and 23). You want the relationship between you and your dog to be understood. Then you can play and have fun.

1 Get a Tug of War toy. This is something that can be easily grasped by both you and your dog. Cloth and cloth toys work very well. You can actually purchase toys designed for tugging. Toss the toy several times for your dog and make sure your dog is interested in the toy.

2 Offer the tug toy to your dog and keep hold of one end. If he won't take one end from you, then toss it, and you take one end from him. Use a phrase to signal your dog to pull, something like, "Who's toy is this anyway?" or "Growl." Growling will entice most dogs to play tug.

3 It is okay for your dog to get or win the toy. After all, that is what Tug of War is all about.
   But first, you need to be able to make your dog "Give" the toy to you if and when you command him to. Teach the "Give" command. (See "Take Me Out to the Ball Game: The Retrieve," Page 24.) If your dog will not give back something, gently twist the toy with one hand and push in slightly on your dog's lips from both sides of the muzzle. Keep your other hand over the dog's nose as you firmly remove the toy from his mouth. Toss the toy again so that your dog doesn't resent you taking it away. It's all right to do this trick on leash the first few times so that your dog doesn't leave with the toy.

4 In controlled Tug of War, *you* start and finish the game. Your dog should not run away with the toy unless you say, "OK."
   A really good game of Tug of War occurs when both you and your dog have successfully won a few games, and the toy has been chased and brought back and played with again and again. Controlled Tug of War has several "Give" commands among the tugs. Play for fun and allow your dog to use up some of his Fight Drive. Tug of War is also great exercise, and this shouldn't be overlooked.
   Tug of War can also be considered a Prey Drive game instead of a Fight Drive game. In Fight Drive, Tug of War is Me against You, with each participant trying to get the toy. In Prey Drive, Tug of War is Me and You against the Tug Toy, and both parties try to "kill" the toy together. Know your dog's drive numbers to see which way your dog is playing Tug of War.

5   As a trick, Tug of War can be part of a skit performed for an audience.
    The skit is played out as you write it. For example, the tug toy might
    be a rubber, rolled-up newspaper and your dog is small or a Toy breed.
    Start the skit with you and your dog fighting over the newspaper. The
    dialogue can be something like, "Get your own paper next time, this
    one is mine." Whatever you think of, dramatically play up the fact
    that each of you wants this one thing. Occasionally, each of you will
    get the item. Have fun with this, and let your imagination be your
    limitation.

Chapter 4

Cute Tricks

Being practical is one thing, but being cute and adorable is where it's at. And what could be cuter than playing dress up with a model whose tail is wagging underneath her clothes? Giving an interview to the best-dressed dog in town is always newsworthy. Watching your dog rolling over or giving you "five" may not serve any useful purpose, but wow, what fun. Here is where to start. Expect to giggle a little. You should probably have your camera ready.

LET'S PLAY DRESS UP

What child doesn't love to play dress up? Well, dogs are no different when it comes to dressing up. And what is cuter than going to the beach with a sun visor on your dog's head or having your dog wear sunglasses during a summertime parade?

Many dogs actually want to wear a sweater in bad weather, and if you have a dog who requires a lot of brushing, you probably want her to wear a sweater also. When you are putting a dog act together, most tricks will seem even more professional if your dog is dressed for the occasion. And think of all the extra treats that you will get on Halloween if your dog goes with you, carrying a sack of her own. A crown, an evening dress, a clown suit—the options are limitless. Remember, let your imagination be your only limitation. *Pack Drive will be of great help when it comes to dressing up your dog. Dogs with lots of Pack Drive enjoy being touched and pampered—they usually tolerate being brushed and groomed without many problems. And wearing clothes is in the same category.*

This trick or treat "Easter Bunny" wins the prize.

1   Your dog should be used to wearing a collar. Get a nice buckle collar and then put it on your dog. If the dog scratches at it, try a distraction. Before you know it, your dog won't mind the collar.

    Take a bandanna or a large handkerchief, fold it in half diagonally, and tie it around your dog's neck. Your dog will look very cool. If your dog accepts this for the day, you are halfway there. If your dog tries to scratch it off, just say, "Stop it," and touch the dog to focus her attention on you. Smile and pet the dog or throw a ball. Change the focus of her attention.

2   Take another bandanna and tie it around your dog's head and knot it loosely under her chin like a scarf. Smile and praise her. Remember to firmly—yet kindly—say, "Stop it" if she tries to tear off the bandanna. Distract her with a treat or another petting session.

3   Get an old pair of sunglasses from the dime store. Getting the glasses to stay on your dog's head will be a challenge. Tie a string to each ear piece and then tie the two strings together, leaving enough room to rest the ear pieces on the dog's ears. The strings will be tied together behind your dog's head, allowing the glasses to rest on top. Now put the bandanna back on your dog's head over the glasses, holding them into place. You now have the cutest grandma in town.

4   Take an old T-shirt or a child's T-shirt (baby size for Toy breeds) and slip it over your dog's head, placing the dog's front legs through the shirt sleeves. It may be necessary to tie a small knot in the shirt at the belly so that your dog's back legs don't step on the shirt. Offer your dog a treat and make her walk to you with the shirt on. Give her lots of praise and make a really big deal over how cute she is. Dogs can be vain. Make sure you give her lots of admiration.

5   Putting socks or shoes on your dog can be a little trickier. They must fit well, as your dog may try to shake them off. On the other hand, you don't want to tie anything onto your dog's feet or legs because you might tie them too tight and cut off her circulation.

    If you have access to baby socks or slippers, use them—they work quite well—even for big dogs. If you have an old pair of knit gloves that you don't mind cutting the fingers off of, you can use these to get your dog used to wearing socks. Be prepared for a lot of laughter, because most dogs will walk like a high-stepping horse, trying to climb out of their socks. Be gentle, and make your dog walk to you for a cookie or another big treat. Most pet stores sell dog boots. These are perfect and can be fitted to your dog.

6   Many pet stores carry clothing items specifically made for dogs. A lot of pattern companies create designs for dogs also, so if you like to sew, you

Your dog will do some high-stepping when he's wearing his boots.

can have the best-dressed dog in town. Once your dog is able to wear and keep the bare essentials on—socks, T-shirts, and bandannas—the rest is up to you.

Have fun and remember to keep your dog's attention on you and not on the clothes. Use food or toys with commands to Come or to Stay. Remember, make your dog happy and pleased to be a fashion plate. *Lots of praise and treats work as distractions for your dog.* Check with your local humane society for any pet celebration days that might have contests for the best-dressed canine. You are bound to get first prize.

MOVE THE NOSE AND THE BODY FOLLOWS

One of the simplest tricks you can teach your dog is to follow something closely with her nose. For example, have her smell a small, aromatic piece of food in your hand. I recommend something like beef jerky. You can also use small pieces of cut-up cheese or anything else that your dog likes. Most important, your dog should be willing to follow the hand that holds the goodie, so the smell should be interesting. When you move your goodie hand, your dog's nose will follow your hand, and then the dog's body will follow her nose. You can't miss. *Dogs with medium to high Prey Drive find these tricks very easy.*

The Interviewer

You can now ask your dog all the questions that you have wanted to know the answers to but were afraid to ask.

1   Move your hand, and you move your dog's nose. Put a small piece of your goodie in your hand, show it to your dog, and let her sniff it. Move your hand directly in front of your dog's nose, going slowly from left to right. Watch her follow your hand in a head shaking motion. Let her have a small piece of the goodie and then try the trick again.

2   Move the goodie slowly from side to side for NO and up and down for YES. Treat occasionally for each response. You can add the commands "No" and "Yes" as if you are confirming the answer you receive. "No? You didn't chase the neighbor's cat today, No?" or "Yes? You do want another cookie, Yes?"

3   To perfect this trick, you must be strong willed. You will want to eliminate your hand as the cue and replace it with your head. Kneel in front of your dog and move your goodie hand simultaneously while you nod or shake your head. Place the treat between your lips or teeth and continue to slowly move your head while your dog watches. Move back and forth for no and up and down for yes. Give your dog the treat directly by hand. Do not spit it out because that will only teach your dog to stop and stare at your face, carefully waiting for flying treats.

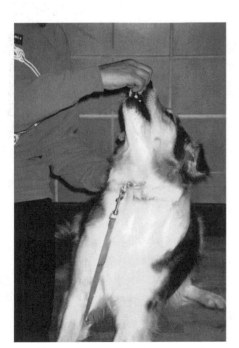

Keep your treat hand connected with your dog's nose.

Sit

It is important to have your dog sit on command, and most tricks require it in one step or another. Sit is one of the most important positions. Dogs with some Pack Drive enjoy the training and the time that you spend with them. They should do well with this trick. *Prey Drive is all about food, so these tricks are easy for dogs with a reasonable amount of this Drive.*

1 Slowly move your treat hand, keeping your connection with your dog's nose, up and over her head.

2 Say, "Sit" in a commanding voice as you move the food at a 45-degree angle over your dog's head. Say it only once, and move SLOWLY to keep the food connection with the dog's nose.

3 When your dog is in the Sit position, praise her with a goodie.

4 Release with OK, or go right on to the next command, Down.

Down

The Down position is extremely valuable when you are establishing a relationship with your dog. (See "The Long Down," Page 20.) *The Down position is also good to be in when sharing time with a Pack Drive dog. You will be using food in this trick, so your Prey Drive dog will love it as well.*

1 First Sit your dog, either with a treat and a command or only with a command. (See the previous section, "Sit.")

2 Say, "Down" as you do the following: Show your dog another small treat and SLOWLY move your goodie hand down toward the ground directly in front of your dog's feet. Round your hand slowly when you get close to the ground,

Move your treat hand slowly towards the ground.

bringing your goodie hand out a few inches in front of your dog's feet. Make it like a rounded L-shape, moving very slowly and *keeping the connection with your dog's nose.*

3 Praise your dog, and give her the goodie.

4 You can release or move on to the next trick, Roll Over.

Roll Over

Rolling over is when your dog lies on the floor and rolls completely over sideways. This is a crowd favorite and gets lots of applause. *Because of the movement involved with this trick, Prey Drive dogs do very well with it.*

1   Place your dog into a Down position either with a command only or with a command and a goodie. (See the previous section, "Down.")

2   Show the dog your goodie hand, and slowly make a small circle around and over your dog's head. Say, "Roll Over." Now circle over and around your dog's head with the goodie. Try to get your dog to look around over her shoulder while lying on the ground by moving the goodie up and over and around.

3   With your other hand, pat the floor beside your dog, and then gently help her roll over in that direction. Try again. Circle around with the goodie, pat the floor, and gently help her roll over if necessary.

Circle the treat and hand over and around your dog's head and shoulder.

4   Make a really big deal about the roll, even if you did all the work. You want your dog to know that the tumble was what you wanted to happen. The only way that your dog will get this message is from you. Get your dog really excited about the roll and try again. *If your dog likes being in Prey Drive, use a high-pitched voice to show your enthusiasm.*

Remember, a dog who is high in Defense Flight might get stuck in the upside-down position. Be very encouraging, and keep your tone of voice low. Watch that you don't tower over your dog when you work on this trick. Keep your body upright while kneeling in front of your dog on the floor.

Sit Pretty

This trick will make even the most mischievous dog look sweet and innocent. This trick will soften any heart. Sitting Pretty is when your dog sits up in a begging position and looks at you with pleading eyes. Pack Drive and Prey Drive are very beneficial for this trick, Pack Drive for the cooperation from your dog and Prey Drive for the desire for the treat.

Who can resist such a face?

1   Sit your dog as in the section "Sit," earlier in this chapter. At a 45 degree angle, lift a goodie over and above your dog's head, saying, "Sit." Remember to move slowly to keep the connection with your dog's nose. Don't feed your dog or give her the treat yet.

2   Instead of giving her the treat, SLOWLY move it an inch at a time straight towards the ceiling. Move *only* an inch at time, trying to get your dog to sit up in a begging position.

3   Say, "Sit Pretty," and keep the connection with your dog's nose. Lift an inch, connect, and lift an inch. Don't go up too high above the dog's nose or your dog will jump for it. You want your dog to *sit* up, not stand up.

Keep the treat connected with your dog's nose and lift it slowly to get your dog to Sit Pretty.

4   After your dog is Sitting Pretty, if your dog knows the word "Stay," you can add it here to help keep her balanced on her haunches. (See "Stay," Page 15.)

Random Rewards

As you teach your dog to follow your goodie hand, give her treats only *occasionally*. Your dog may be getting quite good, even in one training session, but still only randomly reward her with a treat. Make your dog work harder and harder for each treat. Don't stop the treats totally, but rather make each one a true surprise. Eventually, the treat can come at the end of a whole routine after your dog has only followed your hand and listened to your commands.

SNEEZE,"GOD BLESS YOU."

"You are so funny."

Do you realize that your dog lets you know when she thinks something is funny? A dog will sneeze. In a way, it is like a little giggle.

Most likely when your dog meets you at the door in the evening, she will sneeze along with greeting you. When you start to play on the floor or start to interact directly with your dog, you will often get a sneeze for your efforts. Tell your dog a joke, or trip over something, and your dog will sneeze (giggle) at you.

One of the best tricks—one that will impress even your most difficult-to-impress friend—is getting your dog to sneeze on command. You will have to learn a lot of new dog jokes for your dog, but it will be worth it. *Pack Drive is necessary for this trick. It is the Pack Drive that makes your dog see the humor in you.*

1   Find out what makes your dog laugh. Most dogs will automatically sneeze at you when you start trying to get them to do something after a period of not paying any attention to them.

"Yippee, trick training is fun!"

   Get some food and find your dog. Kneel down with your dog in front of you and say, "Sneeze," and then you sneeze *at your dog.*

   Stay totally still with the treat clutched to your chest. Wait. Pretend sneeze again and wait. Wait. If you are starting to look pretty silly, good work. Keep it up!

   When your dog blows *any* amount of air out of her nose—whether it's a full sneeze or a partial sneeze—go crazy with praise and give her the treat. Then do it all again. Remember that to get a full-blown sneeze, you must reward any attempt to sneeze at all. You are looking silly to your dog, but your dog doesn't realize that you actually want her to laugh at you. You need to make it clear to your dog that you really have gone over the edge.

Give tons of silly praise.

To Recap

Kneel in front of your dog.
Hold food in your hand to your chest. Do not offer it to your dog.
Give the command, "Sneeze" and pretend to sneeze at your dog.
Wait, wait, wait.
Pretend to sneeze again.
When air comes out of your dog's nose, give her a treat and tons of praise.

2   Practice Step 1 over and over again. Stop and then come back to it.
     You shouldn't have too much trouble making your dog laugh. Your
     command is, "Sneeze," but most dogs will sneeze *with* you, so practice
     sneezing with your dog.
         Timing is really important to this trick. Your dog must learn that it
     is the sneezing act that you are rewarding. To accomplish this, you must
     praise the *instant* your dog blows any air out of her nose. This is a fun
     trick to teach because you and your dog end up laughing at each other.

3   When a dog sees the treat but cannot get it, the dog becomes excited.
     This will aid in your attempt to get a good sneeze. Once your dog has
     made the connection to give a full sneeze on the command, "Sneeze"
     (which is followed by your pretend
     sneeze), you must always reinforce the
     trick with food and rewards even for
     the slightest resemblance of a sneeze
     from your dog.
         If you do not reinforce the trick
     with rewards, your dog will stop sneezing.
     Be prepared to reward even the little
     blows of air in front of your friends. This
     is very important. It will make the next
     sneeze bigger, not smaller. Good luck,
     and don't forget to practice. It never
     hurts to try this one during allergy
     season!

Humor makes you a team.
Learn to laugh at each other.

HIDE AND SEEK *OR* THE GREAT SAFARI HUNTER

This is more a game that you can play with your dog than a trick. You can spend hours playing with your dog in the house on a rainy afternoon—and you should. Play is exactly what your dog needs for good companionship. But did you know that it is exactly what you need as well? It is a proven fact that owning a dog makes you live longer.

Obviously, Pack Drive is central to Hide and Seek. You can make this a Prey Drive game also, emphasizing the thrill of the hunt. You need to be particularly aware of your dog's Flight Drive because a dog can get very scared upon discovering you if you are not careful. With a lot of Prey Drive you may need to add some motivation to the game, but we will cover that later.

1 You must be able to get away from your dog so that you can hide. *With high Pack Drive dogs this can be tricky because they stick to you like glue.* If necessary, toss a five-second treat—a treat that your dog will not swallow whole, yet also won't lie down to eat and then stay there—into another room and walk briskly to an easy hiding place, (perhaps behind an easy chair that leaves you mostly exposed). A small dog cookie works well as a five-second treat.

Who is looking for whom?

2   Wait a few moments to see if your dog comes looking for you. *Dogs who are very high in Pack Drive will look for you automatically when they realize that you aren't in sight.* If you can peek around a crack in the chair, it is fun to watch your dog look for you. If your dog is not in sight, make a noise—*a whistle or a squeak for Prey Drive, your dog's name for Pack Drive.* Remain slightly hidden.

3   Make sure that your dog comes all the way around the furniture to you when she sees you. Give her a treat reward or a big hug, *depending on your dog's Drives. Your dog's Pack Drive will come alive just by finding you, while a cookie treat will make the Prey Drive in your dog very happy.*
    But here is where you need to be careful. You want your dog to *enjoy* finding you. That is the game: looking for you, and then finding you. If you scare your dog when she finds you—even accidentally— you will discourage your dog from ever looking for you again. Instead, your dog may become nervous when she doesn't see you. She might be afraid that you will pop out of nowhere. *Dogs with a lot of Flight Drive and/or little Fight Drive can become stressed unless you let them find you*

When your dog sees you, make sure she comes all the way around the furniture *to* you.

quietly and reward them with a smile on your face. Say nothing, and let such dogs adjust to you. Dogs with high Flight Drive will love this unless you behave like a jack-in-the-box.

4   Gradually make your hiding places more difficult to find. Start out in the open, then go under the tables, then go behind doors, and finally go to really challenging places such as closets (leaving the door open only a few inches). Let your imagination be your limitation.

To Recap

Distract your dog in one room.
Hide in another room.
Make a noise or call to your dog.
Be quiet, and let your dog hunt for you.
Wait to be found, and then reward your dog for a job well done.

GIVE ME A KISS

As a dog lover, you will want to show affection to your dog. And what is more rewarding than the unconditional love your dog returns? Having a pet can add years to your life. According to the scientific world, a pet's love reduces stress. Now it is time to give some of that love back to your dog. Pack Drive is an absolute necessity for this trick. A dog with no Pack Drive will not want to kiss you no matter what you do. It would be like kissing your little brother or sister—*no way!* So to make sure you are not wasting your time, check your dog's score and make sure there is some Pack Drive—the more the better.

1   If your dog is large, sit her on the floor and kneel next to her. If your dog is small, pick her up in your arms. Either way, make sure your dog is in Pack Drive by petting and smiling at her. Be very careful about your body posture—don't stand up and bend over your dog. Rather, kneel or sit next to her if she is on the floor. *You need to have your dog attentive to you and in Pack Drive to do this trick.*

2   After you give your dog a hug, say, "Give me a Kiss." Make a kiss-kiss sound (smacking your lips) and present your kisser to your dog. If you get no response, make the kiss-kiss sound again. *Don't repeat your "Give me a Kiss" command.* Instead, gently blow into your dog's face and make the kiss-kiss sound. *If your dog's highest Drive is Defense/Fight,*

do not attempt to blow in her face unless you have done the Long Down and Long Sit sections in this book successfully (see Pages 20 and 23).

If your dog gives you a kiss (licks your face), give her lots of praise and let her lick you as long as you wish. Make sure you show praising acceptance of the kiss and do not act upset about your wet face. This will only discourage your affectionate pooch.

What is more rewarding than the unconditional love that you get from your dog?

3   Repeat Step 2 often at different times during the day. Make your dog understands the "Kiss" command so that you can ask for—and get—a kiss at anytime. After all, isn't that a fantasy come true? Ask for a kiss and get a kiss? Okay, okay, it's from a dog, but a rose by any other name would smell as sweet, and a kiss is a kiss. Remember to release your dog and give lots of hugs in return for her kiss.

Problem Solving: If you are unsuccessful in getting your dog to kiss you by putting her into Pack Drive and if a gentle blow of air doesn't work either, it is time to resort to temptation. Very few dogs need this solution, but just in case, here it is. Follow Step 1, but instead of Step 2, lightly put something tasty on the spot that you want your dog to lick (kiss). For example, a touch of butter, peanut butter, or cheese rubbed onto a spot on your face will do the trick. Give the "Give me a Kiss" command and then present your tempting, smelly face. After a short sniff you are sure to get a lick. Remember to praise your dog for the kiss. Repeat until you can use less and less of the tempting substance. Always give a clear command so that you are teaching the command. Praise your dog appropriately, and then release her with lots of hugs.

4 Use your "Give me a Kiss" command between other tricks as part of your act. It serves as a great crowd pleaser, and your dog will view it as a break because of the interaction between you. Getting a kiss and giving a kiss can be a lot of fun, but you probably already know that.

EASTER EGG HUNT

Once a year you can have your dog join in on an Easter Egg Hunt. Or for a more regular challenge, you can play find the cookie and dare your dog to discover a hidden treat. After all, you are not a gumball machine just handing out goodies. Your dog should work at finding her rawhide chew or rope toy. *Prey Drive is a must for this trick. You are teaching your dog to hunt out food. This is exactly what Prey Drive is all about—rummaging for and obtaining food.*

1 Start out with a dry treat that has a good odor, like a slice of dog beef jerky. Put a pile of old newspapers on the floor and spread them out a little. Call your dog to you and show her the slice of jerky. Tell your dog to Stay (see Page 15) and hide the slice between several bundles of paper. Tell your dog it is now time for the hunt to begin. Release your dog from the Stay with an "OK" (release word) and give the "Hunt" or "Find it" command. Encourage your dog to continue looking as her nose begins to investigate the pile. If interest begins to lessen or if your dog is not having a quick success finding the treat, start lifting a layer of the paper to reveal an edge of the prize. *Make a big deal about your dog's success.*

If the find was easy, do it again. If the find was a little difficult, make it a little easier this time and don't put the treat or prize too deep into the pile of papers. By using a high-pitched voice and encouraging words like "hurry," "find it," "you can do it," and "hurry up," you will be keeping your dog in Prey Drive. Because this is needed to hunt for and find food, it will increase your dog's success at finding the "Easter Egg." So keep it up and remember to use a high-pitched voice to elicit the Prey Drive.

2 After hunting through the pile of papers has been successful, try hiding the food elsewhere in the room. Some examples would be in the couch pillows, among the shoes on the floor, and under the throw rug at the door.

This trick is similar to the hot/cold game you may have played as a child. You may remember that if you were close to the item, you were told you were getting hotter, or colder if you were moving away from the item.

You are your dog's coach. Help by pointing and guiding. If your dog is getting colder, use your voice for encouragement. Make it fun for your dog by planning frequent successes.

A word of caution: *Do not hide food on the coffee table.* One of the house rules should be that food on the coffee table belongs to the *people* in the house—never to the dog. You should teach your dog this rule. Do not sabotage yourself by putting accessible food on the coffee table and encouraging your dog to take it.

You should spend some time teaching—*No stealing food from the coffee table.* You can easily do it by simply setting the situation up with your dog. Put a piece of pizza or cheese on the table and have your dog walk by on leash; if she does more than a casual sniff, check your dog with the leash and collar and keep walking. Continue this and sit next to your dog while *you* are eating at the coffee table, but never let your dog have food *there*. If you are consistent and patient, you can teach your dog anything you want to.

3 Impress your houseguests with your Sherlock Holmes Dog who can sniff out anything. Plant an edible dog prize somewhere in the room and call your dog to find it for your friends. This can be great fun for all. Remember to use your Prey Drive voice to aid your Sherlock as Dr. Watson would help when necessary.

At Easter time, boil some eggs and peel them. Hide them during the Easter Egg Hunt for your dog to find. This way it truly becomes a family affair. *Don't let your dog find too many.* We all can eat too much at holidays if we are not careful, so can your dog.

GET IN, GO THROUGH

Now that you can *stop* your dog from crossing a threshold (see "Door Manners," Page 31), the opposite can be just as rewarding. Teach your dog to go *through* an opening. This can be handy for getting your dog in a crate for housebreaking, in hotels when traveling, or at the veterinarian or groomer, as well as for problem chewing. You can use it for many tricks too, like getting the dog to hide under the table or in the following tricks.

Teaching the command "Get in" is very easy. If you have a crate, you can use it, or you can get a cardboard box and lay it on its side. You can also use your closet as long as the floor has plenty of space. You will need some food and a hungry dog. *The higher your dog's Prey Drive, the more your dog will like food training.* Pack Drive dogs may not want to leave you, so make sure you use food they really like to entice them to leave you for the food.

"Get In" or "Go Through."

1   Get your box and your food, and call your dog to join you. Show your hungry dog a small piece of food and toss it into the box. Make sure it is not a scary looking box, *especially if your dog has much Flight Drive.* Say, "Get in," and toss the food into the box, crate, or closet. Do not shut the box, as it doesn't matter whether your dog comes back out with the treat to eat it. The important thing is that she went in to get the treat on command.

To Recap

Say, "Get in."
Toss in the treat.
Praise your dog, and say what a clever dog she is.
Say, "OK," and allow your dog to come out.

Do this several times over the course of several training sessions until your dog willingly runs in to get the treat.

2   Now you *want* your dog to get in *before* getting the treat. Tell your dog, "Get in," and then give the treat after your dog goes into the opening. This will cause her to wait for the treat inside. Hand it in *immediately at first*, then gradually make your dog wait a few extra seconds before getting the treat. You can say, "Wait" if your dog is coming back out immediately. (See "Door Manners," Page 31.)

To Recap

Say, "Get in." Allow your dog room enough to go in.
Hand in the treat after your dog crosses into the opening.
Say, "Wait," if necessary.
Praise your dog as she eats the treat.
Say, "OK," and allow your dog to exit the box.

"Wait" before coming out.

3 You can use this command anytime you want your dog to go through an opening without you going first.

After making your dog *wait* at the car door (see "Door Manners," Page 31), say, "*Get in*," so your dog will jump into the car or onto the wagon tailgate. It is a very useful command.

Let your imagination be your limitation to where and when you use your "Get in" command. To your dog, "Get in" means the same as "Go Through." Don't forget you can use it that way too, to allow the dog to go *through* an opening or *into* a small space.

MY DOG IS A CAT IN DISGUISE!

Cats love to rub themselves on your legs in a figure "8" pattern. This is something that dogs do not typically do on their own, but you can teach your dog to do it. *Dogs with lots of Pack Drive should find this to be fairly easy. A little Prey Drive will help because you can use food to help focus your dog's attention on your hands.*

The command for this trick will be, "Be a kitty cat?" Use this before starting each step of the trick. You will be using your "Get in" command (see Page 70) to teach your dog what to do while learning the trick. Remember that "Get in" also means "Go through." To your dog, these two actions are the same. Going into a box or going through the opening results in the same action; therefore, you use the same command. You also need to think of it as the same to be consistent.

1 Get your dog to Sit and Stay near
   you. (See "Sit Stay" in Chapter 2.) Stand with your legs
   apart and your back to the
   dog. Have small bits of food
   in both of your hands.

      Ask your dog, "Be a kitty
   cat?" Bend forward and show
   your dog a small piece of
   food from your right hand
   between your legs. Say,
   "Get in" (Go Through).
   Your dog should come
   through your legs to get
   the treat. Give the treat
   and praise your clever dog.

Doing the figure "8."

To Recap

Face away from your sitting dog.
Tell your dog, "Be a kitty cat?"
Stand with your legs apart and show a treat with one hand between your
     legs.
Say, "Get in," and tempt your dog through with a treat.
Praise your dog for coming through, and let him have the treat.
Repeat until your dog is willingly walking through on command.

2 Start over and have food in both hands. Command your dog to walk
   through your legs. This time, before giving the treat, guide your dog
   around your right leg with your right hand until your left hand is visible between your legs. Say, "Get in," again. This time offer the treat
   with your left hand after the dog has come through your legs the second
   time. Your dog is now starting to make a figure "8" around your legs.

To Recap

Face away from your sitting dog.

Say, "Be a kitty cat?"

Open your legs and show a treat with your right hand.

Say, "Get in," and tempt your dog with a treat guiding around your right leg.

Show your left hand between your legs with a food treat.

Say, "Get in," and get your dog to come through again.

Praise your dog for coming through and let him have the treat from your left hand.

Repeat until your dog is willingly walking through and around your right leg and through your legs again on command.

3   Continue in the same fashion as in Step 2, except get your dog to go around your left leg too. This will complete the full figure "8" around your legs. Let your dog get the treat after going through your legs three times. The first time to start, the second time after going around your right leg, and the third time after going around your left leg.

Show your dog a treat, and guide her through your legs.

To Recap

Say, "Be a kitty cat?" to start the trick.

With your dog behind you, command, "Get in," and show right hand with food.

Guide around your right leg and then show treat in the left hand from between your legs. Say, "Get in."

Guide around your left leg and show treat in the right hand from between your legs. Say, "Get in."

Praise and release and give your food treat.

Repeat until your dog circles both of your legs without any problems.

4   Keep your dog going around your legs several times without a release word. You may need to give a few small treats while your dog is walking around your legs. This will ensure following your hands as they guide the dog around your legs. That is why you will need to have several treats in both hands.

Keep practicing until your dog understands going around your legs without getting treats all the time. Remember your command, "Be a kitty cat?" Then help your dog get started and use your hands to guide—more as signals than treat dispensers. Make sure you always end the trick with an "OK" release word and lots of treats and praise. *Have fun.*

Guide your dog around both of your legs—first one and then the other.

SERPENTINE WALKER

Have you ever seen a snake weave in and out of weeds? You can teach your dog to weave in and out of your legs even while you walk!

Your dog can walk through your legs and cross through again when you take your next step. By using your "Get in" command, this trick becomes very easy.

This is a Prey and Pack Drive trick because Prey is stimulated by movement (you will be moving, and your hands will be swinging during this exercise), and Pack Drive dogs like working with you—and this trick takes real teamwork.

1   Teach your dog to do the "My Dog is a Cat in Disguise" routine as above.

2   Now all you have to do is to start walking as your dog does the figure "8" pattern around your legs. Don't rush the stationary portion of this trick. Take the transition from standing to walking slowly. After one step, praise and release your dog with a treat. Remember to help guide your dog with your hand holding a treat. Get the focus first on your right hand and then on your left, as you guide the dog around your legs.

Guide your dog around your leg as you step forward and begin to walk.

3   Guide your dog around your right leg. Then, step forward with your left leg and guide the dog around that leg. Step forward with your right leg and guide him around that leg *as you step forward* with your left leg. Release your dog and remember to give a treat and lots of praise.

Gradually speed up so that your dog
walks around your legs as you walk on.

As your dog becomes confident about moving with you, it will not be necessary to bend over as far because the dog will be better able to focus on your hands between your legs. This will be very helpful for your back! (Depending on the size of your dog, this trick can be a real back breaker for you.) A little dog takes lots of bending, but a larger dog takes just about as much because you will be teaching your dog to duck through your legs. Holding the treats lower as your dog comes through your legs will help teach the dog to lower her head as she comes through.

4 Gradually speed up your steps but never *too* fast because your dog needs to make it all the way around your legs with each step. The command you give for this trick is up to you. You can still use "Be a kitty cat," but you are walking instead of standing still. Practice makes perfect. So keep practicing.

HOW DO YOU DO?

It is customary for people to shake hands when greeting. When you greet a dog, the only difference is that you shake a paw instead. *A dog with much Flight Drive will often offer its paw as a communication of submission. When you see a dog roll over completely when you greet it, it is communicating to you that it knows you are more powerful than it is. The step before rolling over completely can be lifting its paw to you. Therefore, Flight Drive can be helpful when teaching this trick.*

1   Tell your dog to Sit. Praise your dog for doing so, but do not give the release command. If your dog didn't Sit on command, simply tuck the dog's tail into a Sit and *praise anyway.* Offer your right hand palm up, so the dog could lay a paw into your hand. Command kindly to "Shake." If your dog sniffs your hand *ignore it.* Slowly reach between your dog's front legs and lift the right elbow. Slide your hand down to the paw and gently cup it in your hand as you shake it. *Praise tremendously* and then release with an "OK," and give either a treat, a big hug, or whatever your dog likes most. Do it over and over until your dog starts to voluntarily lift the leg without any resistance.

"How do you do?"

To Recap

Sit your dog.
Offer your open palm and say, "Shake."
Reach in and lift the elbow of the dog's right leg.
Slide up to the paw and gently shake.
Praise lavishly while you are shaking.
Release with "OK."
Reward.

Do Step 1 many times so that your dog has an opportunity to hear the command, "Shake." Dogs learn through and need repetition before being offered the next step.

2   Tell your dog to Sit. Offer your open palm with the command, "Shake." This time *hesitate* before reaching for the elbow. If necessary, after the pause, gently touch the elbow, but then return to the offered palm position.

Give your dog the opportunity to lift a paw. If the dog voluntarily lifts a paw at all, praise exuberantly and take the paw and shake gently. Then release with "OK," and pet your dog or give a treat. Stay at this level until your dog is lifting the paw off of the ground on command. You then take the paw and shake it as any polite person would do.

Hesitate before reaching for your dog's elbow so that
she will start to lift her paw for a handshake.

To Recap

Sit your dog.
Offer your open palm and say, "Shake."
Hesitate to see if your dog will lift a paw at all.
Reach in and touch the elbow if necessary.
Return to the "offered palm" position again.
When the paw is lifted at all, reach and shake it.
Praise while you are shaking; make sure you have a big smile.
Release with "OK."
Reward, yippee.

3   At this step when you offer your open palm with the command, "Shake," your dog should lift the leg, even if only slightly. Reach for the palm and gently shake as you smile and praise. Then release your dog with the "OK" release word and reward.

To Recap

Sit your dog.
Offer your open palm and say, "Shake."
When your dog lifts her paw, even slightly, take it.
Shake the paw while you smile and praise.
Release and Reward.

GIVE ME FIVE

As I'm sure you know, "Give me five" is when you offer your open palm and someone else slaps it. This trick will work wonderfully if your dog offers the wrong hand while teaching the "How Do You Do" trick. Whenever you offer your open palm and your dog gives you the wrong paw to shake, just say, "*You are so cool. Give me five.*" *High Flight Drive makes this trick easy also.* (See "How Do You Do?," Page 78.)

To teach this as another trick completely, (not just as a saving face response), follow the previous steps for shaking hands, but reach for the other paw and give another command.

1   Tell your dog to Sit. Praise your dog for doing so, but do not release. If your dog didn't Sit on command, simply tuck your dog's tail into a Sit and praise anyway. Offer your right hand palm up, so your dog can lay a paw into your hand.

Aim for your dog's left foreleg, the opposite one from shaking hands. Command kindly to your dog, "Give me five." If your dog sniffs your hand ignore

Make the Give Me Five look like a slap instead of a shake.

it. Slowly reach for and lift the elbow of your dog's left foreleg. Slide your hand down and gently cup the paw in your hand as you let it lay there for a second. Praise tremendously and then release with an "OK," and either give a treat, a big hug, or whatever your dog likes most. Do it over and over again until your dog starts to slightly lift a leg without any resistance.

To Recap

Sit your dog.
Offer your open palm and say, "Give me five."
Reach in and lift the elbow of the left leg.
Slide up to the paw and gently hold for a second.
Praise and smile.
Release with "OK."
Reward.

2 Do as in Step 2 of How Do You Do. Sit your dog. Then offer your open palm with the command, "Give me five." This time *hesitate* before reaching for the elbow. If necessary, after the pause, go in and gently touch the elbow, but then return to the offered palm position. Give your dog the opportunity to lift the paw. If you get the dog to voluntarily lift the paw, praise exuberantly. Take the paw and hold gently. Then release with the "OK" release word, and pet your dog or give a treat. Stay at this level until your dog is lifting the paw off the ground on command.

To Recap

Sit your dog.
Offer your open palm and say, "Give me five."
Hesitate to see if your dog will lift the paw at all.
Reach in and touch the elbow if necessary.
Return your palm to the offered position again.
When the paw is lifted at all, reach and hold it for a second.
Praise and give your dog a big smile.
Release with, "OK."
Reward, hurrah!

3 At this step, when you offer your open palm with the command "Give me five," your dog should lift the leg, even if only slightly. Reach for the paw and gently hold it as you smile and praise. Then release your dog with "OK," and reward.

To Recap

Sit your dog.
Offer your open palm with "Give me five."
When your dog lifts a paw even slightly, take it.
Hold the paw while you smile and praise.
Release and reward.

4   Now you can stop holding the paw for a second to make it look like your dog slapped *your* open palm. Tell your dog to Sit. Praise for the Sit. With the command, "Give me five," offer your open palm. When your dog lifts the *left paw*, put your open palm underneath it, and slide your dog's paw off. This will look more like the "Give me five" action of slapping.

Your dog is a "Cool Cat." It might not be a good idea to let your dog know this, by the way. Some dogs might take offense to being called a cat.

YOU HAVE FOOD ON YOUR NOSE. "I KNOW, I'M SAVING IT FOR LATER."

Balancing food on your dog's nose can be a real crowd pleaser. It can be fun especially when your dog will keep the food there until you say, "OK," and even better when the dog tosses it in the air and catches it before it touches the ground.

"Look Ma, no hands!"

Dogs high in Pack Drive will most likely have no trouble with this. Prey Drive dogs will view it only as an interference between them and the food on the nose. Let's get started.

1 First you need to cup your hand over the top of your dog's nose. Simply Sit and pet your dog for a few seconds, then cup your hand over the muzzle from the top. If your dog accepts this, you will have no trouble with this trick. *A dog high in Defense/Fight Drive will not easily accept this unless the relationship between you is in order. (See "The Long Down," Page 20.) A dog high in Defense/Flight might crumble and lie down unless you are very careful about your body posture. Don't lean too far forward; rather, kneel in front of your dog and lean back a bit on your heels.*

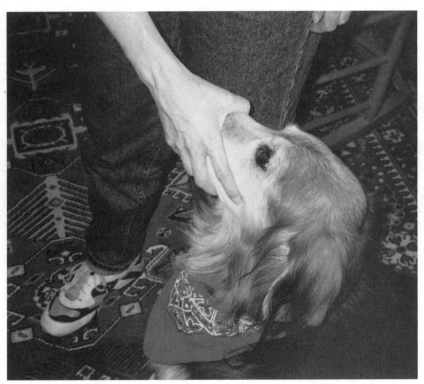

Gently hold your dog's muzzle with one hand and focus
your dog's attention on the food in your other hand.

2   First, Sit your dog in front of you while you are kneeling. Watch your body posture, and lean back on your heels slightly. With one hand, gently hold your dog's muzzle with your thumb on the bridge of the dog's nose and your fingers under the jaw. (If your dog is jumpy, put a finger in the collar first. Then pull the collar up and gently hold the muzzle with your thumb on top, fingers under the jaw, holding the collar too.)

With your *other hand* near the nose, show a small treat and try to get your dog to focus on it. Say, "OK," release your dog, and give the treat. Repeat until your dog is truly focusing on the treat without any struggle.

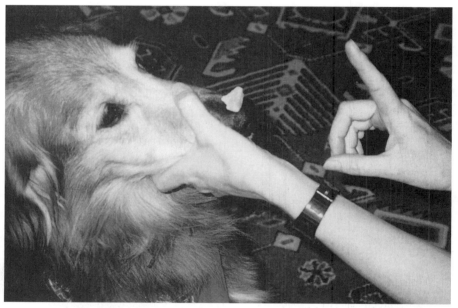

Still holding your dog's muzzle, place the food on the tip of her nose and keep your "Wait" signal in front of your dog's face.

3 Still gently holding the dog's muzzle with one hand, bring the treat
   up with the other hand and slowly lay it on the dog's nose in front of
   your thumb. Keep the treat hand close to and in front of the nose and
   say, "Wait." You can even make it a signal by holding up a finger, as in
   "wait a minute." After two seconds, say, "OK," and let go of your dog
   completely. The treat will either fall off or get flipped up into the air.
   Help your dog find it on the floor and make a big deal about it. Let
   your dog eat it and give lots of praise. What fun!

4 As in Step 2, gently hold the muzzle and slowly place the treat on
   the nose. Add seconds to the "Wait" command and work up to holding the muzzle with your dog balancing the treat for 20 seconds. Keep
   your finger in front of the dog's face until the time is up. Release and
   let your dog find the treat.

   By letting your dog find the treat, the dog will flip and catch the
   treat or quickly move the muzzle away and catch the treat in midair.
   You might end up with a dog that simply drops it and grabs it. Either
   way you will end up with a brilliant circus dog.

Slowly let go of the muzzle after placing the food on your dog's nose. Keep your
"Wait" signal visible.

5 After you set the trick up by gently holding the muzzle and balancing the treat, slowly let go of the muzzle and keep the focus finger in front of your dog's face. Wait just a few seconds, release, and let your dog get the treat. Remember to help your dog find the treat on the floor, if necessary.

6 Gradually make the "Wait" time longer and longer. Gradually move the focus finger farther and farther away from your dog's face. If your dog tosses the treat or drops it before the "OK" release word, you try to get the treat before the dog, saying, "Try harder." Do it over and shorten either the time or the distance.

7 Show off. Try bigger things, like a big milk bone or a ball. *Let your imagination be your limitation.*

Chapter 5

Hollywood Bound

When people have a talent that is worth noticing, they want to show it off—usually for fame and fortune, of course. Dogs are no different. Skill and excellence should not be kept a secret.

Some of the tricks previously mentioned—and all of the tricks that follow—can be worked into an act for your dog that will make talent scouts stand up and take notice. If no one fromHollywood otices your dog, then possibly someone from the local press will. Maybe you'll even get a standing ovation from an audience in your own living room! If that is not enough, pet therapy groups may be in need of your time and your dog's talents. All you have to do is

"How did you do that?"

make your dog a trick-performing pooch and advertise that you are available. You can have fun and do good work at the same time.

THE MAGIC SHOW IS ABOUT TO BEGIN!

Magic always thrills an audience. Your dog, no matter what age he is, can achieve magician's status with little effort. This trick is easy to do in just one training session. It is a rendition of the shell game. The shell game is where someone has three shells and a pea. They put the pea under one shell and then mix up the shells in front of you. You are then to pick the shell that the pea is under. Well, your dog—the great magician—will never get this trick wrong.

Don't hide talent under a barrel.

After one or two tries, he will be able to impress audiences far and wide by always finding the pea, no matter how many times the "shells" are mixed up and repositioned. *A little Prey Drive will make this trick easy to teach your dog. Pack Drive will be helpful to keep him somewhat balanced during training because you will use food in this trick.*

1 First you will need three cheap plastic flower pots. (The ones you get when you buy potted plants or seedlings at the nursery.) To make the trick more elaborate, try to find white flower pots. You can decorate them if you like, but it isn't necessary. If you do, remember that the pots will be upside down for the trick, so decorate accordingly.

   The reason flowerpots work better than shells is that there are holes in the bottom of the pots. Your dog will be using his nose to smell out the food from under the pot. Secondly, you will need dry treats—dog cookies or squares of dog jerky. Cat food works well too because it smells really good to your dog.

2   Place all three pots on the floor and fill your pocket with treats. Tell your dog to "Sit and Stay" behind the line of pots. (See "Stay," Page 15.) Now kneel down on the other side of the pots.

Show your dog a treat and then place it under one of the pots. Tell your dog to "Find it." Let your dog do whatever it takes to get the treat out from under the pot. Dogs usually nudge and paw at the pot. Once the treat is revealed, let your dog eat it and praise him for his success. If your dog doesn't stay, you can get another person to hold the dog back until you give him the command to go. "Hamming" it up can add action to the trick.

"Which one is my treat underneath?"

To Recap

Line up the pots.
Place a treat under one, but do not mix up the line.
Send your dog to find the right pot by saying, "Find it."
Praise and release your dog.

3   The next step is set up the same line of pots between you and your dog. This time, show the treat, place it under one pot, and switch the pots around by one space each. Don't make it too difficult.

To Recap

Line up the pots.
Place a treat under one and move the pot only a space or two away.
Send your dog to find the treat with, "Find it."
Praise and release your magician.
Do this step several times until your dog gets really good at nudging or
    tipping over the pot to reveal the treat.

4   Now you can test the psychic powers of your magician. Set up for the trick and show your dog the treat. Now mix up the pots as much as you like. Stop touching the pots. Then command your dog to "Find it." Yes, your dog is a born entertainer.

To Recap

Line up the pots.
Place a treat under one pot and move the pots around as much as you
    want.
Pause after mixing up the pots.
Send your dog to find the treat with, "Find it."
Praise and release your performer.
Practice.

The paw is *not* quicker than the nose.

5   Now to perfect your act for your show, figure out how you are going to "ham it up" about the great "Magician." You can say things such as:
        Is the hand quicker than the nose?
        This is something never before seen or done in the canine world.
        The one and only, "MY DOG."

Get an audience and try it out. You can even ask the audience to participant—let them guess where the food is hidden before you send your magical dog to find the right one.

Have fun with this trick. You can even charge admission!

HULA HOOP JUMPER

Hula hoops are not just for toning up the waistline. They make great portable jumping arenas for all sorts of entertainment. After your dog can jump through a hula hoop, you can teach him to jump through it with anyone holding the hoop. This trick is a big hit with kids and senior citizens. If you use your dog for pet therapy or school visits, you can't miss. If your dog has lots of energy and needs plenty of exercise, what better workout is there in the winter than conducting jumping sessions inside the house? Jumping is part of Prey Drive. Therefore, if your dog has any Prey Drive at all, you can teach him this trick. The more Prey Drive, the easier it will be to teach.

While your dog is on a leash, coax him through the hula hoop with a treat.

Get a hula hoop that matches your dog's size—they do come in different diameters. If you have a smaller breed, you may want to eventually get several sizes and make it part of the act to keep making the circles smaller and smaller, therefore making the trick tougher and tougher.

1   Lay the hoop on the ground and take your dog over to see and smell it. Don't force your dog to do anything in particular; just let him see the hoop on the floor.

2   Put your dog on leash and walk toward the hoop and then over it. If your dog jumps it, that is okay. If your dog walks on it, that is fine also.

3   Pick up the hoop and rest the bottom edge on the floor while you hold the top.

With your dog still on leash, thread the leash through the hoop and coax your dog through the hoop with the command, "Jump." You can coax him by offering a treat or by touching the floor and smiling. Once your dog makes it through the hoop—even by walking through it—give him lots of praise and a cookie reward. Do this several times until your dog is going through the hoop without much coaxing. Continue to thread the leash with the hoop resting upright on the floor.

4   With your dog on leash, thread the leash through the hoop and raise it off of the floor just a few inches. Say, "Jump," and help your dog hop over the bottom end of the circle, going through the hoop. Remember to reward him with lots and lots of verbal praise and an occasional food treat.

Repeat Step 4 until you are holding the hoop out in front of your dog at eye level. You want your dog to take a few running steps towards the hoop and jump up and through it. Your dog will still be on leash to help guarantee that he responds to the command and has success with the jump.

5   Now that your dog understands how to go through the hoop—and that the command for going through the hoop is "Jump"—it's time to combine steps and create a spectacular trick.

Take the leash off, and present the hoop in front of your dog. Keep it at a level that your dog already jumps through with ease.

Say, "Jump" and allow your dog to jump through. Give him lots of praise and a food treat. Challenge your dog slightly by holding the hoop at different levels for each jump—sometimes at your dog's knee level—sometimes at shoulder or eye level. If your dog is healthy and physically fit, you might want to present the jump one and one-third times your dog's height at his shoulders. Some breeds can easily jump higher—as much as one and one-half times their height. Know what your dog's capabilities are and be fair. Always make sure that your dog will have firm footing when he lands. It is not a good idea to jump on vinyl, hardwood floors, or wet grass. Remember that your dog is an athlete and needs to warm up before attempting a really high jump.

6   Teach your dog to jump while you pivot in a circle, moving the hula hoop around you. Do this slowly at first to see how far you can challenge your dog.

7   If you have a really high jumping dog who takes a broad, stretching leap over the hoop, try to teach him to jump the hoop when it is off the ground—but parallel with it. First lay the hoop down and teach your dog to jump OVER it on leash. Then hold the hoop up off the ground (horizontally) and ask your dog to jump over it that way. You can make your act even more impressive by asking your dog to jump *through* the hoop sometimes and other times, to jump *over* it horizontally.

8   Add a tutu. (See "Let's Play Dress Up," Page 55.) This trick can turn into a real circus act if you use your imagination—and add a net skirt to your dog's waist. Put a crown on your dog's head and now your ballerina is sure to be a crowd pleaser as he jumps through the hoop. Everyone will want a turn holding the hoop!

9   Ask someone else to hold the hoop and teach your dog to jump through it on command. If necessary, go back to Steps 3 and 4 and repeat them on leash while your partner holds the hoop as instructed. Why not add this step to your dog's repertoire? It's great fun for your friends!

Work up to Step 6 with your friend's help. There isn't a child alive who will not want to get your dog to jump through the hoop once he sees you doing it. When another individual holds the hoop for your dog, it changes the trick, so this part needs to be taught. Don't expect your dog to do this without practice—especially if he has a Flight Drive over 30. Teach your dog that it's just fine to do the trick while someone else holds the hoop. Have fun!

10 The most spectacular part of this trick is to get your dog to jump through the hoop after you have added paper. When your dog jumps through the hoop, the tissue paper taped to it will break. What a finale!

Start by taping tissue paper to the hoop with a hole cut in the center for your dog to see through. After the paper is no longer a problem, make the hole in the paper smaller and smaller, until it isn't necessary to have a hole at all. This will be the hit of the act.

Remember that the purpose of the tissue paper is to create a spectacular finish, not to scare your dog. Therefore, be careful when you introduce the paper. If your dog is high in Defense Flight Drive, you might want to skip this step. Be sure you know your dog's limitations.

JUMP THROUGH MY ARMS

If a hula hoop isn't handy (or even if it is), why not get your dog to jump through your arms? This trick is one that you can always readily show off. The only warning is that your dog should be the appropriate size to fit through your arms. It would be dangerous to try this with a really large dog if he doesn't fit through your arms. A friend of mine told her adult Labrador to jump through her arms and ended up with a bruised jaw when the dog obliged and knocked her cold. So use caution.

Jumping is a Prey Drive trick, so a score of over 30 on the test will make this a lot easier. If your dog is high in Defense/Flight, bending over your dog may cause him some stress, so be particularly careful if he has a lot of Flight Drive. After all, you do not want your dog to be afraid. Remember, this should be FUN.

1 First you need to teach your dog the Jump command by using the hoop (see Page 93). It is much easier to teach the Jump command while using an *object* that your dog can jump through rather than one of your body parts. Put your dog on his leash and get a hula hoop. Do Steps 1 through 5 of the hoop tricks. In Step 5, your dog should be jumping the hoop off leash. This is where you need to be *before* expecting your dog to jump through your arms.

2 To review, practice the Jump command several times while your dog goes through the hoop. This is necessary to warm your dog up and refresh the command in his mind. Afterwards, put the hoop down and get your dog's attention with a treat. This puts your dog into Prey Drive, which you want for the Jump command. The treat doesn't reward your dog *before* he does something, but rather it guar-

Get your dog to jump through your arms—you always have them with you!

antees that he will be *ready* to jump by eliciting Prey Drive.

Squat down and check your body posture—don't bend over. Instead, squat and make a big vertical circle with your arms out to the side. Give the "Jump" command and encourage your dog. If your dog doesn't respond, pause instead of repeating the command. Encourage your dog through by tapping your lower arm that forms the circle with your upper hand. Smile and tilt away from your dog again, trying to elicit Prey Drive even more. When your dog jumps through, remember to give him lots of praise and reward him with a treat.

If your dog is hesitant to make the transition from a hoop to your arms, it may be necessary to ask someone to help you. Use a helper's arms as the hoop and put the leash on your dog, threading the leash through your helper's arms. Tap your friend's arms and encourage your dog to jump through.

After a few repetitions, try it again with your own arms. Stop after a successful jump. Do something else for a few minutes, and come back to this trick later. Ending on a good note allows your dog to think about his successful jump. Work at Step 2 until your dog completes the jump every time you offer him your encircled arms to jump through.

3 Next, teach your dog to jump over your extended leg. Kneel on one knee and extend your other leg out to the side.

If you have a small dog, keep your leg straight out. If you have a larger dog—one capable of higher jumps — bend your leg at the knee to create a higher jumping obstacle. Give the "Jump" command and tap your leg. Make a sweeping motion with your arm to encourage your dog over. Give him lots of praise and reward your jumping dog.

If you need to help your dog, remember to give him a treat before you say the command to guarantee that your dog is in the right Drive—Prey Drive. Try using both your left and right legs. Have fun with this.

4   Once your dog can jump through your arms and over each leg, there's no end to what you can get him to jump over—another dog, an item left on the floor—even your kids.

Always remember that you need to review the command and put your dog into Prey Drive first for this trick. If you need to, lead your dog to jump the new obstacle with a leash first, in order to do it correctly. Let your imagination be your limitation.

BOBBING FOR APPLES

This trick is just what it says. You will teach your dog to stick his head into a tub of water to retrieve a prize. It might be the already favorite toy or ball, or it might be something new, like a rock or any dropped item, or it simply can be food. This trick is for dogs who are easily motivated to play or those who like to eat. Most dogs with any Prey Drive fall into one of those two categories. Fight Drive will also help because sticking their head into water takes some doggie self-confidence, which Fight Drive provides.

Things you will need:

- Start teaching this trick with food items that float, like hot dogs, dog or cat food, or dog cookies. Work up to things that sink, like weighted balls or heavy foods—anything that your dog can easily carry.

- A heavy bowl that matches the size of your dog. Your dog needs to be able to reach the bottom of the container comfortably. A five-gallon bucket will eventually work for a Labrador, but start smaller. A mixing bowl works for Toy breeds. The container needs to be heavy enough so that it isn't pushed along when your dog tries to grab the item.

- A water source or pitchers of water.

- A towel or two—if not for you and your dog, *definitely* for the floor.

Let's get started. Start at a time when your dog is hungry, not right after a meal. Because you will initially be using food, your dog will need to be motivated by the food. And as you know, food is not very motivating after a big meal.

1   Set your container on the floor with towels underneath—no water yet.

2   Drop a piece of food in and say to your dog, "Go Bobbing." You can also use a fetch term like, "Go get it," but since you are teaching your dog a new trick, you will probably want to use a new command. Start with "Go get it" if your dog needs help understanding what you expect from him. But don't worry—dogs learn quickly. Let your dog get the food and give him lots of praise for taking it. Then say, "OK" and really make a fuss over your dog.

3   Repeat until your dog is diving into the empty container for the food.

4   Add an inch of water. Do not use very much water because you don't want your dog to go under water yet. Drop your food and say, "Go Bobbing." Make a really big deal about your dog's fishing the food out of the inch of water. Your dog has just accomplished a great task. Let your dog know how pleased you are.

5   Stop and take a break. Since your dog is getting the food each time, you want to end when your dog is still wanting more.

6   On the next training session, repeat Steps 2 and 4.

7   Add another inch of water. Increase the depth of water slowly. Unless you have a water baby, your dog will need to get used to opening his mouth under water. Floating food will make grabbing it slightly frustrating if the food gets pushed away, so help your dog if necessary. Push the food toward your dog, and hold it steady in the water. Remember to make a really big fuss about any success.

8   Gradually add water to your container until the amount of water is not an issue. *Always end a training session when your dog still wants more.* Don't let him get tired and bored.

9   Go back to Step 4 (only an inch of water), except use something that will sink. Different types of food will sink, or try a ball if your dog really likes to play with them. Continue going through the steps, gradually adding water.

Remember to keep the size of your dog in mind and to keep it fun. *If your dog is high in Flight Drive, do not progress too rapidly or lose your patience.* Teaching something new can be stressful to a Flight Drive dog, and he won't learn if he's too stressed. Quit practicing and do something fun with your dog.

10 Whenever your dog balks at putting his head under water, stop and go back one step. You must add the water gradually in this trick—very gradually for some dogs. At any point you can start to show off your dog's "Bobbing Trick." Your dog need not completely immerse his head for you to have a real crowd-pleaser. Half of this trick is your showmanship. So show off your dog with flair.

DANCE THE NIGHT AWAY

Fred and Ginger have nothing on a dancing dog. With just a few simple lessons you can have the dance partner that you have always dreamed about. Your dance may not resemble the waltz or the two-step, but it will be spectacular in every way. Prey Drive will give your dog the motivation to learn to dance, and Pack Drive will make him a willing partner. Let's have some fun.

1 As you learned in "Move the Nose and the Body Follows" (see Page 57), you can manipulate your entire dog simply by controlling his nose. Get a morsel of food and position your dog into a Sit (see Page 58) by moving the food close to his nose and then up and backwards *slowly*.

Say, "Sit." Give your dog the treat. Instead of releasing your dog from the Sit position, connect the scent of another piece of food with your dog's nose and slowly lift the treat straight up above your dog's head.

Command your dog to "Dance." As your dog stands up, lift the food higher and higher until your dog is standing only on his hind legs. Some dogs are better balanced than others, so be patient. Give the treat after just a second of success so that your dog gets the idea and will do it again. Each time, try to make your dog stand longer, increasing the time only by seconds. Release with "OK" and a treat.

2 Once your dog is standing all the way up on his hind legs and stretching for his food on command, it is time to teach him to really dance.

Remember that before you give the treat, release with "OK" and then feed your dog. This will teach your dog that the "Dance" command, rather than the treat, is the cue.

Tell your dog to "Dance" and move the food treat in different directions—forward, sideways, backwards, forward again, and so on. Keep your dog up on his hind legs for as long as possible, but keep in mind your dog's balance and body build. Be fair and patient. Always release your dog and then give him a treat.

3 You can add a second command, "Twirl," to your dancing dog. The Twirl command asks your dog to spin while on his hind legs and then to dance in a circle. Simply make small circles with your hand or the food above your dancing dog's head and say, "Twirl." This is quite spectacular once your dog learns what you mean. The only way for this to happen is for your and your dog to practice.

To Recap

First command "Dance." (Raise your dog to his hind legs.)
Move your dog around for specific amount of time.
Command "Twirl." (Guide the dog around in a circle.)
Give the Release command and let your dog drop to the floor. Reward.
Repeat again. Dropping and treating can become part of the dance.

4 Dress for the occasion. A tux or a tiara can be very fitting. (See "Let's Play Dress Up," Page 55.) By adding a dancing wardrobe, your dog can look like a Spanish Dancer, a Ballroom Dancer, a Hip-Hop Dancer— you name it. And you should dress to look the part as well. Let your imagination be your only limitation.

DIE, MONGREL, DIE

Playing dead is an old favorite from way back. The whole trick consists of aiming your index finger and "firing" at your dog, with the dog falling to the floor pretending to be dead. Playing with guns is never a good idea, but playing with a loaded finger is usually not too dangerous. If your dog doesn't "Die" on the first command, you can always plead that you are a poor aim or that your finger malfunctioned.

Defense/Flight Drive will make this trick easy to teach. Most dogs who have high Flight Drive (30 or higher) are willing to lie down and roll over to show their belly. This is the "play dead" position. When your dog rolls over and shows his belly without a command, it is usually because you have elicited the Defense Drive—either with your body language or your voice—so that your dog is in Defense/Flight. A dog high in Fight would not naturally exhibit this behavior, so you will have to teach him the roll over first.

1 Review the Down command and the Roll Over command from "Move the Nose and the Body Follows" (see Page 57).

2 If you have a smaller dog, kneel and bend forward toward your dog. If your dog is larger, bend over at the waist. *Remember you are trying to elicit Defense Drive.* First, give the Down command, but do not release your dog from the Down position. Hide a piece of food in your "gun" hand. With a deep, low, strong voice, say, "Bang."

With your gun hand, point down and directly at your dog from above, as you give the strong "Bang" command. A dog with high Flight Drive will roll upside down. With your gun hand, show and give the treat while the dog is still upside down. Then, with a loud, happy voice, release your dog with "OK." This should help your dog get out of the Defense/Flight Drive mode in order to get up and play as a reward.

To Recap

Down your dog.
Hide a piece of food in your "gun" hand.
Use bent-over body posture and a strong, deep voice.
Say, "Bang." Make it sound like a gun shot.
Give the hidden food from your "gun" hand.
Release with "OK."
Play with your dog to get back into Pack Drive from Flight Drive.

If your dog does not collapse into Flight Drive, keep the gun finger pointing and show the treat in that hand over your dog's head to get him to roll over. Be sure to use your other hand to keep the dog from rolling over all the way. Give the treat from your "gun" hand. Try to keep your dog in the "dead" position for a few seconds. Then release with lots of enthusiasm.

3   Now you are going to do the same as in Step 2, except not from a Down position. When you have your dog's attention, you can use his name if necessary or your body posture and a deep tone of voice. Now give your dog the "Bang" command to die.

   Of course first load your "gun" with a treat in your hand. Use the same techniques as in Step 2 to help your dog to get in the roll-over position. Some dogs will lie completely on their backs with their feet up in the air. Others will simply lie on one side. It depends on the amount of Defense/Fight and Flight as to which "dead" position your dog uses. Don't worry about this. The "Bang" command makes your dog drop "dead." That's the result of being "shot." After all, dead is dead. You can't be sort of dead. Whether on the side or on the back, your dog is play-acting "dead." So don't forget to say, "OK" to bring him back to life.

4   Now that your dog will "die" from any position, it is time to teach "dying" from other angles. To do this, gradually reduce your amount of body posture so that you elicit Defense/Flight Drive. Because you will practice shooting often, your dog will quickly learn what the "Bang" command means. That way, you won't need to use so much body posturing to drop your dog. Make a gradual reduction in the degree that you are bent over. If your dog stops dying on the first "Bang," simply back up some and bend over again more carefully. Don't rush to eliminate it so quickly. We know your aim is not that bad, and you should always be able to shoot your dog on the first try. Although you can save face during a performance by claiming your aim is bad, try not to purposely teach your dog that your aim is bad. Happy shooting.

ALL-STAR CATCHER

As you know, catching something takes real hand/eye coordination. In other words, it takes skill. With dogs it takes equal skill, but instead of hand/eye coordination, it takes mouth/eye coordination. With this skill you are going to teach your dog to catch food and then balls or a favorite toy. This trick will

Catching takes mouth/eye coordination.

require some Defense Fight, enough so that things flying through the air do not scare your dog. It will be helpful to have some Prey Drive—enough to want to catch food at least. More Prey Drive will help for catching balls and toys. Pack Drive will help to keep your dog in an attentive sitting position.

1   You will start by teaching your dog to catch a treat or a small piece of food. You can begin with nuggets of your dog's dry food or small pieces of dog cookies. If these items are not interesting enough, use cut up jerky treats or small dots of cheese. Most dogs aren't too picky.

Start with your dog facing you in a sitting position. (See "Move the Nose and the Body Follows," Page 57.) Step back from your dog about one to two feet. Have several pieces of food in your hand. Take one piece and show it to your dog. Then toss it UP a few inches over your dog's head as you say, "Catch." If your dog catches it, you are a very good pitcher. Your skill is getting the piece of food to fall, in sight, slowly towards your dog's face. By tossing the item up first— rather than directly at your dog—the food will move more slowly, and your dog will have more time to focus on it. Also, it will be in the air a little longer, giving your dog a better chance to catch it.

It is better to focus your dog's attention on your hand by showing him the treat and then tossing it upwards on the FIRST hand motion. If you make several pretend tossing motions before throwing the food, your dog will not be able to tell exactly when the food leaves your hand. This will make the trick much too difficult, and that is not your intent. Help your dog to focus, then toss upward with your catch command.

When your dog misses the treat, let him find it on the floor so that you can regain his attention more quickly. If you try to grab for the missed treat, most dogs will continue to look for it, knowing they missed out on a food particle. There are few dogs who will not get to it before you do anyway. True, there is valid philosophy in not allowing your dog to get a dropped treat, allowing him to only eat the caught ones. This philosophy is intended to reward only his successes. But by rewarding the *attempts*—letting your dog get the dropped ones too— you will keep your dog's attention a lot longer, and it will be a lot more fun for you both. Most dogs will grasp the trick a lot faster when they catch their treats and don't have to spend time hunting for them afterwards.

If treats are bouncing off of your dog's nose consistently, watch to see if your dog is shutting his eyes as the food comes close to his face. *This may be a product of Flight Drive.* In this case, toss the cookie so that it lands in front of your dog instead of on your dog, so your dog has a chance to watch where it lands. After his eyes open to watch more closely, gradually get the cookie closer and closer until it is land-ing right on your dog again. By this time, your dog will realize it is okay to keep his eyes open, and you can increase the odds of your dog catching the cookie.

Another problem that can add to lots of missed catches is if the size of the cookie is too small. Try using something a little bigger like a jerky square. It is soft enough not to make your dog duck, but big enough to see well.

2   Now that your dog is catching easily, try to make it more challenging. First distance yourself from your dog. Say, "Catch," and back up a few extra feet. Toss the treat three to four feet away from your dog instead of just two feet. Try again. Keep the distance and say, "Catch" as you make the long toss. Some dogs will focus more closely if they are told to sit before being allowed to catch. As your tosses get farther and farther away, your pitching skill may deteriorate. In that case, your dog will have to get up to hunt. If this gets too embarrassing, let your dog stand so that he can move more quickly and continue to catch the cookie. This makes an even more impressive trick. What looks like fancy throwing may actually just be fancy catching. Your dog will understand.

3   Once your dog understands the "Catch" command using food in his training sessions, it is time to have him catch other things. It is not a good idea to switch from edible to inedible items in the same session. Your dog may feel cheated and may not attempt to catch the item after the first switch.

Toss a different item—such as a tennis ball—for your dog to catch.

Make the catches more challenging.

Instead, start your new session with a ball or a favorite toy. Snowballs can be great fun to catch for some dogs, so be creative. Just make sure it is safe for your dog to catch the toy. Begin with a distance toss. Sit your dog, back up a few feet, show your dog the ball and say, "Catch." Then toss the ball. Make a really big deal about the catch and call your dog to bring the toy back to you. Have your dog give you the ball. (See "Take Me Out to the Ball Game: The Retrieve," Page 24.) Now sit your dog again, say, "Catch," back up, and toss the ball out a few feet. Keep trying until your dog is focusing on catching the ball.

This trick is great for school visits and pet therapy sessions at nursing homes. Your dog can catch and bring back a ball without running through the halls. Other grown-ups or kids can toss food or balls to your dog as well. Your trick training can open a lot of doors for you and your dog.

PUT YOUR HEAD DOWN

This is the sweetest of all the tricks. If you have a little dog, this can be accomplished while holding the dog in your arms. When you give the dog the command for "Head Down," the dog's head will drop onto your chest or shoulder and everyone in the room will get teary-eyed and say, "Aw." If your dog is on the floor and you give the command, "Put Your Head Down," his head will move down, his eyes will look up, and everyone in the room will think that you have the cutest dog in the world. On a personal note, this is the trick my dog was doing when the man who became my husband realized that he loved me. Needless to say, I think this trick is a good one. It worked for me.

This is a Pack Drive trick because it takes maximum cooperation from your dog. Any dog can learn this trick, but if you have a dog with much Defense/Fight, do the Long Down exercises (see Page 20) first. Actually, your dog will need to be able to do the Down and the Stay for this trick, so practice both.

1   Put your dog in the Down position on the floor. If you have a toy breed, you can do this trick on a table to make it easier on your back. Praise your dog for doing the Down, even if you helped put him into position.

2   Command, "Put Your Head Down," and guide your dog's head to the ground with your fingers. Point to the spot between your dog's front paws while you *gently* apply a little pressure to the top of your dog's head with your other hand.

3   Keep your hand on top while the dog's head is on the floor, but remember to do it gently. Praise your dog quietly while you are doing this. It is important your dog

Don't just lie down—lay your head down also!

understands that you want him to have his head completely down. After five seconds, say, "OK," and let the dog get up.

4   Do Steps 1 through 3 again. This time try to relax the gentle pressure holding your dog's head against the ground as you quietly praise him. Relax the pressure, then replace it if his head comes up even slightly. Praise while the head is completely down, but stop praising if the head comes up. After gently placing the head down again, start praising your dog.

To Recap

Praise while the head is down, even if it is with your help.
Stop praising if the head starts to raise up when you relax the pressure.
Place the head down again. Praise.
Relax the pressure, and praise only while your dog's head is down.
Reposition his head if it comes up and start praising him again.
So on and so on. Head down, praise. Head up, say nothing.

It is the praise at exactly the appropriate time that teaches your dog what you are after: that is, the dog's head solidly on the floor. Practice until no pressure is required to hold your dog's head for at least five seconds. Release your dog frequently, but only if the head is completely down when you give the release word.

5   Now it is time for your dog to put his head down on command without your help. Start with your dog in the Down position. Command "Put Your Head Down." Point to the ground as in Step 2. Do not apply your hands to his head, and wait for a few seconds. If your dog's head does not go down, then help him as in Step 3. Don't repeat the command, simply help. Your dog will catch on if you have been practicing praise correctly.

6   Once your dog is able to put his head on the ground by command, you can try this trick with your dog in your arms. Hold your dog in any way that is comfortable for both of you. Command, "Put Your Head Down." Gently touch your dog's head to your shoulder or any body part. Praise and cuddle. (Pack Drive dogs love this exercise—and so do Pack Drive people!) Practice.

Now it is time to invite close friends over to show off the bond between you and your dog. As my husband later explained to me, "That was so special, I just wanted to be a part of that warmth."

Wanting to be part of the
bond and the warmth.

TAKE A BOW

After all is said and done and your performance is over, you must graciously accept your due applause. It is hard earned and greatly deserved. A humble performer takes a deep bow to thank the audience for their warm, heartfelt attention. So, needless to say, you and your dog must be ready for some applause. First of all, your dog needs to be able to Down on command. It is also helpful for your dog to know the Stay command. (See "Long Down," Page 20, and "Stay," Page 15.)

1 First teach your dog the Stand command. Say, "Stand," and with your dog on your left, put your right thumb in his collar and hold the front half of your dog steady. Then put your left hand under your dog's belly and push his hind legs backwards with your left hand. Praise your dog while he is standing and then release him with "OK."

Now review the Down command by telling your dog to Down. Help him into the Down position if necessary. Praise and then release with your "OK" release word. Review both the Stand and the Down command again.

Keep your left hand under your dog's belly and lower the front half of the dog with a treat (Prey) or with a slight pressure (Defense).

2 Stand your dog and then praise for the Stand, but don't give the release. Keep your left hand under your dog's belly as for the Stand command in Step 1.

Put your right hand in the collar under the dog's chin and apply a little pressure toward the ground and say, "Take a Bow." Lower the front half of your dog, and while applying the pressure under his chin, press towards the dog's elbows so that they bend rather than lock against your pressure. If necessary, use a food treat to lower the front end of your dog. (See "Move the Nose and the Body Follows," Page 57.) Hold this position while you giggle your praise. Release your dog and make a really big deal over how wonderfully clever he is, even if he only did a half bow.

Your dog will improve, and that is what counts. Each time he gets better, give him more praise. If he doesn't get better or improve, then don't praise him as much. Just say, "Let's try harder." Then try again next time to help your dog improve. That's the way to let him know what you are striving for—front half down, back end up—take a bow. What a good dog!

3 Stand your dog on command and praise him. Keep your left hand under your dog and pat the ground in front of him while you say, "Take a bow." Hold your left hand there to keep your dog's rear end up. After his front end is down, try to relax your left hand under his belly. Keep it nearby in case his back end slips lower. Your bows must be deep—that means your dog's back end must be high. Remember to release and give him appropriate praise and rewards.

4 Stand your dog next to you. Command, "Take a Bow" and point to the ground in front of your dog. If necessary put your left hand under the dog's belly. Tell him to, "Stay." Take your hands off the dog and praise him. If your dog gets out of the bow position, stop praising and reposition him *into* the bow. Then start your praise again. It isn't necessary to reprimand him at all, just position your dog into the bow again. Praise once more. After a few seconds, release your dog by saying, "OK." Practice this step until it isn't necessary to help your dog at all.

5 Prepare for the applause to become a standing ovation! You can bow too, if you like.

FINAL NOTE

As you practice with your dog, remember that you both share a relationship of mutual trust and affection.

- The more your dog respects you, the more your dog will love you.

- The more time you spend with your dog, the more he will want to spend time with you.

- The more you play with your dog, the more fun you will both have together. So make your training sessions enjoyable.

- Always end on a positive note so that you both look forward to future trick training sessions. Share your patience with your dog, and he will show you what a good trainer you are. A magnet on my refrigerator says: "May I always be the kind of person my dog thinks I am." Now you can be that kind of person too.

"May I always be the kind of person my dog thinks I am."

Glossary

The AKC: The American Kennel Club is a registry of breeds recognized in the United States. The AKC keeps records of bloodlines as well as titles earned by dogs in their registry. The AKC is the governing body for Conformation Events in the United States. They set the rules, approve the events, and govern at the competitions.

All-American: Mixed breed dogs are often referred to as mutts, but it might be better to name them All-American dogs because America is a melting pot of many different nationalities—just like mixed breeds.

Body Language: Body language is a powerful way to communicate with your dog. Learn how simple body motions affect your dog's Drives. Bending over your dog stimulates Defense Drive. Tilting backwards and lifting your arms stimulates Prey Drive. A neutral body posture—kneeling next to your dog—stimulates Pack Drive. Be aware of your body. If you are not careful, you may give off signals that are different from your spoken commands.

Breed: The canine species is composed of many different breeds, each of which each has a Standard of perfection. The Standard usually includes specifics for appearance, function, and personality.

CGC (Canine Good Citizen):   The American Kennel Club has a simple test for dogs that can be given by Obedience instructors and others in your area. It tests the dog's skills for being a Canine Good Citizen. The CGC certificate is recognized by some as an indicator of a dog's manners. There are facilities that will only allow entrance to dogs that have a CGC certificate. The Canine Good Citizen Test evaluates your dog's ability to be under control, walk on a loose leash, follow a few simple commands, and not be too disturbed by distractions.

Check: A check is the use of the collar and leash on your dog. A check is a short motion or a quick pull that is IMMEDIATELY released so there is no more pressure on the collar. After the check—which if done correctly should *gain* your dog's attention—you need to do something to *keep* your dog's attention, like praise her.

Come: The Come command should be used consistently to bring your dog directly and immediately to you. Ideally, your dog should sit when she gets to you, but it is up to you whether or not you teach that step of the Come command. If the command is taught as a pleasant one, your dog should learn to come quickly and happily. You also need to work on the Come command with distractions, so that your dog will come no matter what is going on. "If you don't have a dog that comes when called, one day you won't have a dog."

Command: The command is the cue word that tells your dog to start an exercise or an action. The command should be spoken (or signaled) clearly.

Command/Motion Sequence: It is important that you always give your command before you start a trick or exercise. Give the command before you go into motion. If you start before you command, you are expecting your dog to read your mind.

Communicate: To communicate is the ability to be understood by another. When communicating with another species (dog/human), you need to be consistent and aware not only of the spoken word, but also the tone of your voice, facial expressions, body language, and physical movements.

Correct: To correct is to show your dog what you expected, but the dog did not do. For example, if your dog is jumping on you for a greeting, to correct this behavior you need to show your dog that you want her sitting *on the floor* for the greeting. Correct your dog's behavior by showing her the right action.

Crate: *See* Kennel (Crate).

Defense/Fight Drive: These are behaviors that come from a dog's natural instinct for self-preservation. Some common Fight Drive behaviors are guarding territory or belongings, willingness to investigate strange new things, or not liking to be petted or groomed. Fight/Drive behaviors are activated by the need to defend one's self, prey, or territory.

Defense/Flight Drive: Dog behaviors that show a dog's natural instincts for self-preservation with the concern for well being. Flight/Drive is activated when your dog feels insecure.

Dewclaw: The dewclaw is the fifth toe on the inside of a dog's leg. The dewclaw is generally of no use and therefore is usually removed. In some breed Standards, it is specifically mentioned as necessary for that breed to perform her original function. The dewclaw is comparable to our thumbs.

Distemper: Canine Distemper is a highly contagious virus that attacks the gastrointestinal and respiratory tracts. It can ultimately cause neurological complications. Vaccines for this disease have mostly eliminated it.

Distraction: A distraction is anything that takes your dog's attention away from the task at hand. There are different degrees of distractions. A *first-degree* distraction is anything that might be going on in your area but isn't directed at your dog while your dog is working or training. For example, working in the front yard with regular street activity would be a first-degree distraction. A *second-degree* distraction acts directly towards your dog. For example, someone kneeling nearby, talking sweetly, or asking your dog to come visit them. *Third-degree* distractions occur when food is offered in order to tempt the dog away from the task at hand. It could also be a Frisbee flying overhead or a ball tossed near the dog. *Fourth-degree* distractions are whatever is most distracting to that dog's personally. For example, to a guarding breed, someone approaching from a distance would be a fourth-degree distraction. For a very high Pack Drive dog, someone touching or petting her would be a fourth-degree distraction. It all depends on the dog. You must train your dog to be able to work in spite of distractions. Be patient and show her that whatever is distracting her isn't going to affect the task at hand.

Dominant: Another way of looking at Defense/Fight Drive. The higher the Fight Drive, the more dominant the dog.

Dominate: To dominate is to boss or conquer. This is not the best way to work out a relationship with your dog. Dominance will not produce the mutual respect desired in a relationship between you and your dog.

Down: The Down should be used consistently as a command to get your dog to lay down and remain still. When dogs are given a position command, they should not move from that position until given a release word like "OK."

Drives: Drives are different groupings of behaviors that your dog exhibits. These behaviors are instinctive and are broken into three different categories: *Prey Drive*, *Pack Drive*, and *Defense Drive*. Defense Drive is further subdivided into Fight/Drive and Flight/Drive. It is the concentration of these Drives that make up your dog's personality.

Drop on Recall: This is an exercise that stops your dog from coming while en route to you. When given a "Down" command, your dog should drop to the ground without taking additional steps towards you. It is useful, for example, if something dangerous is in your dog's path. When done formally, this is an exercise in Open Class Obedience.

Dumbbell: A dumbbell is an article that dogs retrieve in the Obedience show ring. It usually is a dowel with a block on each end of the dowel. The dog carries the dumbbell by the dowel. It can be made of wood or plastic.

Fecal: A fecal is a stool sample that your veterinarian would check for the presence of worms or worm eggs. Most veterinarians will want a fecal sample brought in when your dog comes for her yearly checkup.

Flea: A flea is a very prolific external parasite that lives in your dog's hair coat on the skin. A flea bite can make your dog itch and scratch. When your dog chews at the flea, one of the fleas might be ingested, and this can cause tapeworms. Severe infestations of fleas can also cause anemia because fleas suck blood when they bite your dog.

Halter (Face) Collar: A halter collar is similar to a halter for a horse and is worn on the face of the dog rather than on her neck. This type of collar is used to move the nose of a dog with the idea that where the nose goes, so goes the rest of the dog. Dogs need to be introduced to halter collars in a positive manner so they aren't frightened or startled by it. You should never yank on the leash while using a halter type collar.

Heartworm: A heartworm is an actual worm or parasite that lives in a dog's pulmonary artery and heart chambers. Heartworm can kill a dog if there are enough worms to block the passage of flowing blood. Heartworm is transmitted by a mosquito bite, so it is very prevalent in areas where mosquitoes are.

Heel: The Heel command should be used consistently to help your dog into position at your left heel. Heel can be a moving command while walking so that your dog walks along at your left side—no matter what direction you travel or turn into. It can also be used as a command to get your dog to move from somewhere else and *come* to your left side.

Herding Dogs: This Group of dogs are bred to direct stock animals. Some herding breeds are the Belgian Sheepdog, Border Collie, Smooth Collie and Rough Collie, German Shepherd Dog, Puli, Shetland Sheepdog (Sheltie), and Welsh Corgi (Pembroke and Cardigan).

Hock: The hock is the joint between the knee and the toes on a dog's hind leg. The space between that joint and the toes is also referred to as the hock. Appropriate angles are evaluated when a breed's conformation is discussed.

Hounds: The group of dogs that are bred for hunting by use of sight or scent. Some examples include: Scenthounds (Dachshund, Basset Hound, Bloodhound, Otterhound) and Sighthounds (Greyhound, Beagle, and Whippet).

Isolate: Dogs are very social animals, especially those with a lot of Pack Drive. Isolating your dog can be used as a powerful consequence if he is too excited or out of control. But when a dog is isolated too often and for too long, it can cause stress and boredom—and this can result in destructive behavior or worse. Spending more time with your dog can easily rectify isolation.

Jumps: There are three basic types of jumps. A High Jump is a solid jump— usually one and a third times the dog's height at the shoulders. A Broad Jump lays on the ground in sections. It is usually twice as long as the High Jump is high. A Bar Jump is simply a stationary bar that the dog must jump *over* rather than go under. It is usually the same height as the High Jump.

Kennel (Crate): A crate is an enclosure that your dog fits into comfortably and can be used when you are unable to be with your dog. Your dog thinks of her crate as a den or a bedroom. *It is not a place of punishment* but rather a napping opportunity. The size of the crate or kennel should only be large enough for your dog to lie down and turn around. *Your dog will not be exercising in it*, so keep it small enough to allow her the sense of security that goes with a den (a small enclosed shelter).

Leadership: In the natural Pack order, there is always a leader. The leader should be fair and respectful toward subordinates. With you and your dog, *you should hold the leadership position*. But remember to be fair to your dog so that the respect flows in both directions.

Leash: A leash is a length of material used to keep your dog with you. It should be made of something that you find comfortable and easy to handle. It should not be too long or too awkward. Leashes should be kept folded up in your hands so that nothing flaps in the wind (which would stimulate Prey Drive).

Leg: Leg is a term used to describe a qualifying score for any Obedience title. Each title requires three legs. People can often be heard saying, "My dog has two legs towards the Novice degree (CD)."

Long Down: A Long Down is similar to a Time Out with children. It is a leadership exercise that establishes your relationship with your dog. It is not a Stay exercise but rather a way of showing your dog that you make all the decisions as to where, when, and for how long your dog will do something. It is a simple, fair way of showing leadership in a manner that your dog understands. This exercise will improve your relationship with your dog.

Long Sit: *See* Long Down. The only difference is that the Long Sit is done in the sitting position for a different length of time.

Match: A Match simulates a Dog Show or Obedience Trial but is not actually the real thing. A Match is run like a Trial but is practice to see where you are in your training and to have the experience of showing. A Fun Match can be put on by anyone, and you can train in the ring if you wish. A Sanctioned Match is one put on by a club associated with the AKC; you are not supposed to train in the ring, just like at a real show.

Mites: Mites are an external parasite that live on the skin. Ear mites live in the ear and can cause ear infections. Mange mites live on the skin and cause baldness and sores that can get infected. See your veterinarian for diagnosis and treatment of mites.

Motivate: To motivate is to get your dog to do something willingly through inducement or the removal of force.

Name Proof: To Name Proof your dog during training is to teach your dog to wait for a command following her name. Your dog's name is not a command, simply an attention-getting device used before commands.

No: This is a negative command used too often for too many things. It should not be used this way. Instead, No should be replaced by appropriate commands that redirect your dog in a positive manner. For example, if your dog is not allowed on the furniture, say "Off" instead of "No," and then direct your dog to the floor.

Non-Sporting Dogs: The group of dogs bred to be companions. Some examples include: Boston Terrier, Chow Chow, Dalmatian, Keeshond, and Lhasa Apso.

Novice (Companion Dog [CD]):   A Novice Obedience title is obtainable through different agencies like the AKC. It is the first level of Obedience. To earn this title, your dog will need to Heel on and off-leash, do a Recall, and perform other exercises.

Obedience: Obedience is the sport of showing your dog's skill in working with you. There are three levels of Obedience: Novice, Open, and Utility.

Object of Attraction: An object of attraction is anything that dogs like enough to follow closely with their noses. Usually a small piece of food works well, but it need not be food. A toy may have the same power of moving your dog's nose.

Off: Should be used consistently as a command to move your dog when her paws are somewhere they should not be. This command should be used instead of "Down"—*not the appropriate command if you are being consistent.* For example, when you come home and your dog jumps up on you, tell your dog "Off," and then redirect your dog into a sitting position for an appropriate greeting.

Open (Companion Dog Excellent [CDX]):   CDX is an Open Obedience title obtainable through different agencies like the AKC. It is the second level of Obedience. To earn the CDX title, your dog will need to Heel off-leash, Drop on Recall, retrieve, jump, and do other precision exercises.

Pack Drive: Pack Drive is the set of behaviors that shows a dog's willingness to be part of a pack or group. Some common behaviors exhibited in Pack Drive include getting along with other dogs or humans, enjoying being petted or groomed, and following their person around the house. Pack Drive behaviors are activated by group hierarchy and by being with others.

Parvo: Parvo is a highly contagious virus that attacks a dog's gastrointestinal tract and can quickly dehydrate the animal, resulting in death. The signs of this disease are bloody diarrhea and vomiting.

Pet: A PET IS A FAMILY MEMBER. A pet should have the benefits of being part of a family as well as the rules and limitations of being in a family group. A PET SHOULD BE FOR LIFE.

Praise versus Petting: Praise and petting are not the same thing. *Praise* is when you TELL your dog how clever she is. You should use a very happy, pleasant voice that your dog responds well to. *Petting* is when you bond with your dog. Petting should take place AFTER your dog is done working, and praise should occur WHILE your dog is working.

Prey Drive: Prey Drive is the set of behaviors that show a dog's natural instinct for obtaining food. Some common Prey Drive behaviors are sniffing the air or ground, stalking things in the grass, stealing food, digging, and so forth. Prey Drive behaviors are activated by sight, sound, and smell.

Prong Collar: A type of training collar that has individual links distributing the force of the correction around the dog's neck. It allows the trainer to use less force to get the dog's attention than do some other types of training collars. It should not be used unless an owner has been taught professionally how to administer corrections with a prong collar.

Quick Stop: Quick Stop is a brand of styptic powder most often used to stop bleeding when you cut your dog's nails too short. When nails are trimmed too closely, the quick will bleed. You should always have styptic powder handy when you clip your dog's nails.

Random: When you use food as a training inducement, you need to offer it only as a special reward for a job well done. Do not give food for every performance, dispensing it as if you were a gumball machine. As your dog becomes better trained, you will be able to praise with your voice and then give her food for a job particularly well done. Your dog's performance will improve if she's given food randomly, not constantly.

Recall: The recall is a term used to describe the exercise at a dog show. The dog is left on a Sit Stay off leash and about 35 feet away. The dog is then called and comes to sit in front of her owner.

Registered: To have a registered dog is to have papers (a certificate) from a certified registry, like the AKC, or through a breed club proving that the dog is purebred.

Regression: When your dog learns something new, you can often observe a period of regression in her skill. This usually occurs at five to six-week intervals during each training period. Be patient—this is a normal part of learning for any dog. Always end each training session with a positive experience, whether your dog is having a regressive experience or not.

Reinforce: To reinforce is to strengthen an association between two things. For example, to reinforce a Sit Stay, you would put your dog back into position if she moves from the sitting position. This reinforces the Stay command with the Sit position.

Release: The release is the word you give your dog at the end of each command. If you tell your dog to sit, for example, your dog should remain in the sitting position until released. After the release you should always give your dog a reward. *See* Reward.

Rescue Dog: A rescue dog has usually had a previous home or no home and is now being placed into what will hopefully be a permanent home. Rescue Dogs can have special needs and can make great pets.

Respect: A dog should not be completely overpowered but rather respected, just as you should be respected by your dog. To have a relationship of respect with your dog is to live in harmony.

Reward: A reward is compensation for a job well done. A reward can be anything your dog likes—a smile or a pat for a dog with lots of Pack Drive— a treat or a ball for a dog with lots of Prey Drive.

Scent: The word scent usually defines use of the dog's nose while hunting or for locating an item. Dogs can discriminate for scent much better than we can.

Self-rewarding: Accomplishment is its own reward. For example, to a high Prey Drive dog, retrieving can be so much fun that you don't need to give a treat for the dog's performance. Having retrieved is reward enough.

Sit: The Sit command should be used consistently to get your dog to sit and sit still. A dog who is given a position command should not move from that position until she is released with a word like "OK."

Slip Collar: A slip collar is a training collar that slips and tightens and then slips and loosens with the use of the leash. A check on the leash tightens the collar; a slack leash loosens the slip. Also sometimes wrongly called a choke collar. The slip collar can be large enough to go over the dog's head but then will rest too low on the dog's neck. Or the slip collar can snap around the dog's neck, helping it stay higher on the neck and therefore making it more effective.

Smile: A smile is the facial expression that you should use frequently when you are with your dog. Smiling at your dog is the body language for praise. When you find your dog looking at you, remember to smile back.

Sporting Dogs: Sporting Dogs are those in the Group bred to hunt. For example, all Pointers, Retrievers, Setters, and Spaniels are Sporting Dogs.

Stand: This command should be used consistently to get your dog to stand up and stand still. When given a position command, your dog should not move from that position until she is given a release word, like "OK."

Stay: This command should be used consistently to get your dog to be completely still and not move from a particular position. The dog becomes a statue, and only her head or tail can move, but nothing else that is touching the ground. Stay must have a clear release word signaling that the Stay is over, for example "OK."

Stop: The Stop command should be used consistently to get a dog to quit doing something. It should replace the word "No," which is overused and too negative. The *Stop command should be followed by a redirection*. For example, if your dog is chewing on the rug, say "Stop" in a firm voice, and then redirect your dog's chewing by giving her an appropriate chew toy.

Stress: The way your dog's body reacts to either mental or physical demands is called stress. Under stress, the body becomes chemically out of balance. Signs of stress can be panting, pulling back the lips in a smile-like grimace, or even leaving sweaty paw prints on the floor. Make sure your dog has exercise, a stable environment, and fair and humane treatment so that stress will not be a part of her life.

Submissive: Submissive means low Fight Drive. Submissive behavior also results from inhibited Flight Drive if a dog cannot run and freezes in position or rolls over, exposing her belly.

Tab: A tab is a short, mini-leash that hangs from your dog's collar. It can help you reach for your dog after you remove her regular long leash.

Tapeworm: Tapeworms are internal parasites that live in a dog's intestines. They are contracted by ingesting fleas or killing rodents. You can see the tapeworm segments in the dog's stool (fecal sample)—they look like rice or sesame seeds. Tapeworm is easily treated, so see your veterinarian (who will probably ask you to bring in a fecal specimen).

Terriers: Terriers are the Group of dogs that were bred to hunt vermin. Examples include: Airedale, Scottish, West Highland White, and Cairn Terriers.

Therapy Dog: Dogs can be used in therapy for all sorts of people. The young, old, handicapped, and sick can all be cheered up by the presence of a dog. A Therapy Dog needs to pass a series of tests to be certified. Check with your local training center for someone in your area who offers this test.

Ticks: Ticks are external parasites that attach to your dog's skin. Usually, they are barely big enough to see, but if left alone, they can suck enough blood to become swollen to the size of grapes. Ticks can carry disease and should be removed safely with tweezers so as not to break off in your dog's skin.

Title: A title is an official designation given by a registry to a dog receiving an appropriate amount of points or legs for a specific activity. Examples include Champion, Companion Dog, Companion Dog Excellent, and so on.

Tone of Voice: Your voice alone can change your dog's Drive; a soothing quiet voice for Pack Drive, a quick, high pitched voice for Prey Drive, and a loud, low, harsh voice for Defense Drive. Make sure you use the appropriate tone of voice when communicating with your dog.

Toy Breeds: Toy breeds are the Group bred for small size and companionship. Examples include the Affenpinscher, Chihuahua, Pomeranian, Toy Poodle, Yorkshire Terrier, and Shih Tzu.

Training Collar: A training collar is used with a leash to connect you to your dog. When used correctly, it will get your dog's attention. Training collars can be anything from a regular buckle collar or a slip collar to a halter face collar made of various materials.

Treat: A treat is a small piece of food given to your dog as a reward. It should be big enough to be enticing, but so small that it is instantly gone.

Trial: A Trial is a show held by an official licensing organization for points or legs towards Obedience titles.

Utility (UD): Utility is an Obedience title and obtainable through various licensing agencies like the AKC. It is the highest class level of Obedience. To qualify for the Utility title, your dog needs to do Hand Signals, Scent Discrimination, jumping, and other precision exercises.

Wait: The Wait command should be used consistently to tell your dog not to progress or move forward. It is not a Stay, during which your dog can't move. Rather, a stay is a command to *not* go ahead with something just yet, for example, to *not* go through a doorway.

Withers: Withers are the highest part of the shoulder blades, right behind the neck. This is where a dog's height is usually measured.

Working Dogs: Working dogs are the Group bred to do a specific job. Examples include the Akita, Alaskan Malamute, Boxer, Doberman Pinscher, and St. Bernard.

Index